WRITING INCISIVELY
DO-IT-YOURSELF
PROSE SURGERY

WRITING INCISIVELY
DO-IT-YOURSELF
PROSE SURGERY

WILLIAM STRONG
Utah State University

McGraw-Hill, Inc.
New York   St. Louis   San Francisco   Auckland   Bogotá   Caracas
Hamburg   Lisbon   London   Madrid   Mexico   Milan   Montreal
New Delhi   Paris   San Juan   São Paulo   Singapore   Sydney   Tokyo   Toronto

for Carolyn and Robert

Writing Incisively:
Do-It-Yourself Prose Surgery

1 2 3 4 5 6 7 8 9 0   DOC DOC   9 0 9 8 7 6 5 4 3 2 1

ISBN 0-07-062270-1

This book was set in Aster by Arcata Graphics/Kingsport.
The editors were Lesley Denton and David Dunham;
the designer was Jack Ehn;
the production supervisor was Annette Mayeski.
R. R. Donnelley & Sons Company was printer and binder.

Library of Congress Cataloging-in-Publication Data

Strong, William (date).
   Writing incisively: do-it-yourself prose surgery / William
Strong.
       p.   cm.
   Includes index.
   ISBN 0-07-062270-1 (text). — ISBN 0-07-062411-9 (IM)
   1. English language — Rhetoric.   2. Editing. . I. Title.
PE1408.S7716   1991
808'.042 — dc20   90-23611

ABOUT THE AUTHOR

William Strong directs the Utah Writing Project and teaches courses in writing, reading, and English education at Utah State University. In addition to many articles and book chapters, he has written several textbooks published by McGraw-Hill—among them, *Sentence Combining: A Composing Book* (1973, 1983), *Sentence Combining and Paragraph Building* (1981), *Mastering Basic Vocabulary* (1984), *Practicing Sentence Options* (1984), and *Crafting Cumulative Sentences* (1984). His computer software includes *Storyspinner* and *Word Stories* (Wasatch Education Systems, 1986). He is a frequent presenter at NCTE conferences and sites of the National Writing Project. In 1988 he received an award for teaching excellence at Utah State University. He likes to ski, sail, and ride motorcycles in open country.

ABOUT THE ARTIST

Jerry Fuhriman is a professor in the Department of Landscape Architecture and Environmental Planning at Utah State University. His watercolor landscapes of the intermountain west and desert southwest have won several major awards and now hang in many corporate as well as private collections. His eclectic interests include silversmithing, sculpture, and the fanciful style of drawing shown in this book.

CONTENTS

AN IMPORTANT NOTE TO INSTRUCTORS

A brief Instructor's Manual for *Writing Incisively* is available, free, from the College Department at McGraw-Hill, Inc., 1221 Avenue of the Americas, New York, NY 10020.

This manual contains a teaching rationale and an answer key for "Do-It-Yourself Exercises" in the text. Answers are in the form of easy-to-use transparency (or photocopy) masters for large-group instruction.

A basic premise underlying this self-teaching textbook is that given-language exercises provide *one* way for students to develop insights about revising, editing, and proofreading tasks. According to Lev Vygostsky, the great Russian linguist who postulated a "zone of proximal development" in language learning, whatever learners can do with structure, they can eventually do on their own.

A second key premise is that revising and editing exercises are an adjunct to real writing, not a substitute for it. Hence, the "Personal Application" exercises following each of the six chapters—three on revising, three on editing—should be part of each learner's routine. Students should be encouraged to apply principles of "reading with care" in workshop settings that encourage collaboration and peer response. Demonstrations of "Prose Surgery in Action" result from such workshops.

To provide classroom context for work on revising and editing, the Appendix offers a single in-depth writing assignment (pp. 235–250), plus many practical suggestions for *generating* and *drafting* text. Whether you decide to use this assignment or ones of your own design, please emphasize with students that the Appendix serves as a prewriting reference. Begin with the Appendix if students need help in generating and drafting papers; otherwise, turn to the interior chapters—the heart of the writing process.

ACKNOWLEDGMENTS

It's been over twenty years since I sat in the late Francis Christensen's writing class at the University of Nebraska. For me, his words still ring true. They echo throughout this book but especially in Chapter 2, with its emphasis on levels of paragraph development.

Donald Murray's influence also runs deep, particularly his insistence on careful reading, writing for one's "best self," and the craft of prose surgery. I owe much to this great and gentle teacher—as do others in our profession. Master surgeon that he is, he has shown us all how to probe for meaning and let the text make its own diagnosis.

Several reviewers helped me develop my ideas about revising and editing. They included Noreen Fiacco, Eastern Nazarene College; Jessie Garner, Pace University; Mark Harris, Jackson Community College; Virginia Heringer, Pasadena City College; Dennis Jochins, Lake Sumter Community College; Kathleen Kraeger, Walsh College; Dolores Schriner, Northern Arizona University; Bill Smith, Virginia Commonwealth University; J. T. Stewart, Seattle Central Community College; Tom Waldrep, University of South Carolina; and Mindy Wright, Ohio State University. I sincerely appreciate their thoughtful readings of the manuscript.

Finally, I offer friendly thanks to Will Pitkin, whose insights into prose structure I often appropriate as my own. Kudos also go out to my colleagues in the National Writing Project, whose work continues to inspire and inform, and to teachers in the Utah Writing Project, who keep me on my toes. Like it or not, this book belongs to all of you.

William Strong

WRITING INCISIVELY
DO-IT-YOURSELF
PROSE SURGERY

INTRODUCTION TO PROSE SURGERY

> *Surgeons must be very careful*
> *When they take the knife!*
> *Underneath their fine incisions*
> *Stirs the Culprit—Life!*
>
> —EMILY DICKINSON

The purpose of this book is to help you develop revising and editing skills—hence, its title, *Writing Incisively*. **Incisive writing** is text with a clean cutting edge. Since *revising* and *editing* refer to moves you make to achieve that edge, you might think of this book as a do-it-yourself guide to prose surgery.

Now that you see the book's point, let's cut to the heart of the matter. The simple truth is that writing looks easy when you're *reading* it. Take right now, for example. Making your way through these opening paragraphs, you probably don't care that it took someone two years to write them. You cannot see my yellow legal pad with many pages of false starts or my green computer screen where words were rearranged, added, or zapped with the *delete* key. And you cannot hear me clearing my throat, trying to find the right voice.

All you see is the final written product, the words flowing left to right across the page, the ideas neatly arranged. And all you hear is one voice, not the voices from previous versions of this text. Consider yourself lucky not to be dealing with the earlier clutter or listening to the mumbling of other voices. Whatever you sense as an edge of truth or authority results from my work with earlier drafts.

Because the surface of finished writing looks smooth and seamless, many of us get the mistaken idea that writing well is simply a matter of deciding what to say and then saying it. Such thinking is a dangerous trap. Why? Because when we discover that incisive writing is not quite as easy as it first appears, we start thinking that something is wrong with *us*—that we're stupid or "just not the writer type." We put ourselves down for no good reason. And then we give up.

The fact is this: It takes time and effort to produce clean, interesting, and easy-to-follow prose. This is true for everybody, not just for you. Unfortunately, the surface of text—black against white—reveals nothing of how it is made. So trust me when I say that skilled writers mainly "hang in there"—reading and revising, rereading and editing. They listen to their writing as they imagine others will, and they use certain surgical skills to help their meanings emerge. Those skills—revising and editing followed by careful proofreading—are what you'll learn about and practice here.

What you also need to understand is that writing usually evolves from rough notes to one or more drafts and, eventually, to the final text. Teachers and writers call these evolving stages the **writing process.** While this process may seem a bit mysterious at first, it's far less difficult than learning to speak a first language—a task you mastered long ago. The more you understand the process of writing, the better prepared you are for prose surgery.

WRITING PROCESS PREVISITED

To begin with a "slice of life," I'll make a small but true confession, one of waking up to early morning darkness while writing this Introduction. Although writing before daybreak isn't my usual pattern, this particular morning found me listening to the quiet of the sleeping house, the murmur of the river out back, and a voice composing itself inside my head.

An hour or so later, with the slumbering shapes of furniture beginning to emerge in the predawn darkness, I finally got up. Outside stood the dark mountains, outlined by a thin, silvery edge of light. I drove downtown for coffee and a steak-and-eggs breakfast—not exactly health-food fare but one that felt right.

What I had in mind was to rework the opening of a finished book on revising and editing. My aim was to provide a glimpse of the person *behind* the words and to show how revision—in this case, adding new material—felt to him. It wasn't easy. I had an idea or two to get started, but the writing began to smooth out only as I recalled the advice of my mentor and friend, Donald Murray. "Lower your standards," he growled from my memory, quoting the poet William Stafford.

So I tried not to worry about how the new sentences would mesh with what I'd already written. "You can cut and fit later," I told myself. "And you can always revise the revision."

My writing was interrupted only by the steak-and-eggs platter, coffee refills, and dawn above the mountains. As I scribbled away, trying to capture a tentative voice within, the light slowly changed from the color of charcoal to a soft rosy-gray. I was working for what Murray calls "velocity," a kind of relaxed momentum in the act itself—like skiing or running or riding a motorcycle. When you're *into* these activities, the experience takes over. The same goes for writing.

It was risky to write such a personal introduction—I knew that—but I was attracted by the challenge. Could I tell the truth about how I approached revision? Could I communicate my nervousness about what to say next? If so, maybe my book would be *read* with care. And wasn't that what I was after—to write truthfully and incisively?

The café draft took well over two hours, not counting the hour I had spent earlier trying to get back to sleep. The prose surgery that followed on the computer screen took much longer, spaced out over several days. The paragraphs before you—ones that now take only moments to read—bear little resemblance to the original draft. Trust me when I say that the ideas and sentences have undergone major reconstructive work. I only hope that my incisions and sutures are invisible—or nearly so.

I tell you all this for three reasons.

First, I want to stress that composing is unpredictable for everybody, you and me included. For example, my motivation for revision was actually a telephone call from my editor, Lesley Denton, who suggested I might want to "think about" revising the book's introduction to include more context for my ideas about revision and editing. Like any writer, I mumbled agreement and then moved on to other things. Little did I realize that my subconscious self had taken up Lesley's challenge and then set to work trying to figure a new angle. As usual, rethinking led to some interesting surprises. "Way leads on to way," as Robert Frost once put it.

Second, I want you to know that not knowing where you're going—only half-seeing the emerging shape of what might be written—is a typical experience. Contrary to what many people think, good writing rarely springs elegant and full-flowered upon the notebook page or computer screen. Instead, it emerges from notes, crossed-out words, and interruptions, arrows pointing this way and that. Like you, I may hear an echoing line or have a vague sense of what I want to say, but my ideas are often shadowy—like the shapes of furniture and mountains in the just-before-dawn darkness. It's always an act of faith as I follow hunches, hoping to "see the light" sooner or later.

Third, I want to emphasize that incisive writing *can* be learned—if you're willing to let your emerging text show you how. But opening yourself up to what you've written means reading from a different angle, from the viewpoint of someone reading your words for the first time. Your struggle as a writer—including the realization that what you thought was finished is being revised yet again—really doesn't matter to your reader. What matters is how your words cut through the reader's boredom or confusion to make sense of a subject. To create this edge, you listen carefully to hear what needs to be said, and then listen again. What matters most is patience. There are—pardon the pun—no "shortcuts" to writing incisively.

Having said that writing incisively takes time and effort—and that the process is unpredictable and messy and requires close attention—I must also add that I took real *pleasure* in reworking the sentences from the café. I've cut through these words dozens of times, trying to see the underlying meaning and feel the direction that the text itself wanted to take. Each change led to others.

I have the feeling that as I carefully reread what I've written, new words will suggest themselves. In fact, they are doing so right now as this sentence unfolds itself left to right across the page. Like you, I am both reader and listener, wondering what the text is trying to say—the purposes it has. But only *I* know how these words have sprung from within and were revised, again and again. Perhaps the poet Paul Valery was right to say that writing is "never finished, only abandoned."

MAKING SENSE OF THE WRITING PROCESS

There are many ways to think about the writing process, and some are less useful than others. Consider this pair of particularly simpleminded and backward ideas:

Step 1		Step 2
Study grammar rules	$\longrightarrow$	Write a perfect paper
Make a complete outline	$\longrightarrow$	Write a perfect paper

Research suggests that merely studying rules is a dead-end approach to writing. People learn to write by writing—and by reading their written work with care. In other words, you learn grammar from writing, not the reverse. As for outlines, most writers don't use them. They're far too busy making rough notes—then writing and revising—to worry about complete outlines *or* perfect papers.

While we're on the subject of approaches to writing that *don't* work, here are two more that you may have heard about (or practiced) in your schooling:

Step 1   Step 2
Write a first draft   ⟶   Kiss up to instructor
Wait for inspiration   ⟶   Make creative excuses

The first approach is demeaning, the second desperate. Both avoid the real issue—*learning*—and put the focus on pleasing a teacher to get a good grade. If such strategies didn't work for you before, why should they work now?

On the surface of it, the following diagram appears to make more sense. Compared with the ideas above, it seems to have some logic behind it.

Think ⟶ Write ⟶ Change ⟶ Correct

Unfortunately, this method of writing distorts matters. As my experience in the café makes clear, writing is not a lock-step process. In adding new material to a finished manuscript, I wasn't so much "correcting" my work as completely rethinking and reshaping it. I was extending and clarifying what I had already done, not *fixing* it.

Perhaps a better explanation is provided by the diagram below, one that outlines two connected cycles of the writing process. Cycle 1 centers on the steps for shaping up various drafts of a text; cycle 2 centers on steps for "shipping out" the final product. Taken together, these two cycles describe a sequence of general behaviors for people who write, yourself included.

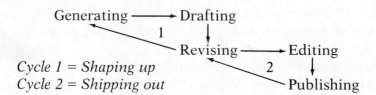

Cycle 1 = Shaping up
Cycle 2 = Shipping out

In generating, you may develop lists, make word clusters, draw diagrams, ask questions, talk with others, read background material, jot down outlines, or use free writing to get your ideas flowing. Often called *prewriting*, the generating step builds energy for writing. While to others generating may seem like "fooling around," nothing could be further from the truth. As you generate ideas, you feel their energy.

In drafting, you probably select ideas, decide on a tentative plan, and start your sentence-by-sentence composing. An early draft of your text may have logical gaps, shifts in direction, and several errors in spelling, usage, or sentence construction. For the time being, however, such problems are not important. The draft—a step in the larger process—gives you something to work on. It get you moving.

In revising, you reread your draft to examine its details and support, organization, and continuity—the flow of development. You imagine yourself as an eventual reader, listening to the text and asking whether it makes sense. You focus on what's being said. As you see and sense new possibilities, you go back to the generating stage for more words, fresh connections, or better organization.

As the diagram makes clear, thoughtful revising lies at the heart of the writing process. Put literally, **revising** means reseeing or "seeing again." Writer William Zinsser says that "revising is the essence of writing"—and many writers agree. When you revise with care, your text is teaching you what it can become.

Skilled writers often loop through cycle 1 several times before moving into cycle 2. Sooner or later, however, they decide that their prose is basically "shaped up" and now needs to be put in better form so that it can be "shipped out" and shared with others.

This shift of intention puts the focus on editing. In this step, you spot and fix errors, tighten language, and rearrange words for emphasis. Editing differs from revising. When you edit, you focus more on the *form* of language and less on the content or organization. Editing is an effort to "get things right"—to consider *how* something is said. Editing gives the final "edge" to your text.

As the diagram makes clear, the editing stage leads to some kind of publishing—more specifically, preparing a final copy, proofreading it carefully, and sharing it with an audience. Making photocopies for a peer response group is a kind of publishing. So is sending a letter to a friend or preparing a term paper. In your writing class, the audience may include not only your instructor but also other students.

Why does cycle 2 show an arrow pointing from "Publishing" to "Revising"? For two reasons. First, getting work published—whether in school, the world of work, or your personal life—often requires that you revise your "final" copy, sometimes making major changes. In fact, such revisions may even take you back to the generating step. Second, published work sometimes goes through a series of editions. Rewriting already published work—your personal résumé, say—provides yet another chance to "get it right."

So the preceding diagram shows a way to work smarter, not harder. Think about it: *Instead of trying to get everything correct in a first draft, take things a step at a time.* Most of your revising and editing will probably occur *after* your draft is developed, not while it is evolving. This should reduce your frustration—and speed up your writing—because you won't be trying to do too many things at once. You will focus your attention instead of dividing it—a smart strategy.

Does this mean you should avoid making changes while drafting a paper? Of course not. On-the-spot changes occur naturally as your ideas emerge. The point is that doing major surgery *too early* can cut you off from your best thoughts. What some people call "writer's block" can result from an overeager surgical hand: Phrases, sentences, and even whole paragraphs will be crossed out or thrown away, leaving you with a wastebasket full of tattered beginnings and nothing to work on.

In addition to the right timing for prose surgery, remember Anne Tyler's words about its difficulty: "It takes courage to cut, to simplify, to reveal meaning. It's easy to obscure meaning in a swamp of language, but to cut everything away reveals the meaning and exposes the author."

Simply put, then, learning to revise and edit on your own means learning prose surgery. The aim of this book is to help you develop a number of skills that you can apply to your writing in progress.

HOW THIS BOOK WORKS

Writing Incisively is a self-teaching textbook. Its six chapters focus on revising and editing methods, the art of prose surgery; the Appendix outlines helpful strategies for generating and drafting prose.

In the Appendix you'll also find a writing assignment. Use this assignment as raw material for the Personal Application exercises in the six chapters, unless your instructor provides other writing tasks for your revising/editing practice. If you're unsure of yourself as a writer or need how-to-do-it tips to get started on writing assignments, *read the Appendix first.*

With one or more writing drafts in hand, you're ready for the heart of the book, these six chapters on revising and editing:

Part I: Reading to Revise

1. Reading to Revise: Writing More Fully

2. Reading to Revise: Finding Logical Order

3. Reading to Revise: Tinkering with Paragraphs

Part II: Reading to Edit

4. Reading to Edit: Seeing Sentence Connections

5. Reading to Edit: Trimming Flabby Sentences

6. Reading to Edit: Correcting Sentence Errors

While the book focuses mainly on revising and editing at the paragraph and sentence levels, please note that the first three chapters provide essay-length contexts for your learning. All of the illustrative paragraphs are part of larger essays, on the topics of procrastination, model schools, and memory.

As noted above, these six chapters explore the heart of the writing process, whereas the Appendix offers you practical help for generating and drafting ideas. The Appendix thus serves as a kind of reference. Use it when you have trouble getting started on a paper or when you need to work up new material during revision.

Each chapter has its own set of exercises (with built-in answers) designed to teach you a range of revising and editing skills. For best results, check the answers *after* you do the work. Following each chapter, you'll find four more Do-It-Yourself exercises for additional practice, plus a Personal Application activity. Your instructor will supply answers for the Do-It-Yourself exercises.

You'll also find, at the end of each chapter, a section called Prose Surgery in Action. Each of these sections shows a college student working to revise and edit, using prose-surgery techniques demonstrated in the chapter—for example, *adding details and support, cutting unneeded material, reorganizing, using transitions, trimming flabby sentences, proofreading,* and so on. Seeing how someone else uses these techniques will help you revise and edit your own work; study their surgical moves.

The first chapter, "Reading to Revise: Writing More Fully," deals with key questions that can help you generate added details and support. The chapter shows you how to work with underdeveloped prose and how to guide the reader's attention with strategically placed transition words and phrases.

In Chapter 2, "Reading to Revise: Finding Logical Order," you'll learn two basic frameworks for paragraphs. This chapter reveals the beneath-the-surface structure of paragraphs and invites you to reorganize (and delete) material at different levels. It thus helps develop and expand your earlier learning about asking questions.

Chapter 3, "Reading to Revise: Tinkering with Paragraphs," provides more practice in adding, deleting, and reorganizing sentences to improve prose structure. You'll learn six basic patterns for making (and combining) paragraphs. And you'll see that disorganized ideas—even good ones—make for less-than-effective writing.

The fourth chapter, "Reading to Edit: Seeing Sentence Connections," deals with sentence-to-sentence coherence. An "x-ray approach" shows you how sentences hang together as paragraphs. By studying the cohesive links between and among sentences, you'll improve the flow, or "connectedness," of your prose.

In Chapter 5, "Reading to Edit: Trimming Flabby Sentences," you're invited to cut through wordiness and vagueness. The real goal of this chapter is to reduce confusion. Eliminating the "clutter" in sentences leads to thinking more effectively; and better thinking, most teachers agree, leads to better writing.

Chapter 6, "Reading to Edit: Correcting Sentence Errors," provides practice in editing and proofreading. In school, proofreading can mean the difference between a low grade and a high one; and in the world of work, proofreading can determine everything from whether you get the job to whether you keep it. This chapter helps you "sweat the details."

Finally, of course, there's the Appendix, which is designed to help you generate and draft your ideas both in the early stages of writing and later on, when extending your thinking in new directions. In everyday life, you may be able to live without an appendix; in your life as a prose surgeon, however, you'll probably need this one.

READING WITH CARE

Now that you have an overview of the book, let's consider a skill that underlies *any* effort to revise or edit prose. That skill is reading with care. It's a skill not often taught in school—in fact, the emphasis in school is sometimes just the reverse—yet it's a skill that practicing writers acknowledge as fundamental to their craft.

How do you develop this skill?

Caring about what you write is the starting point. If *you* don't care about what you say and how you say it, why should anyone else? An indifferent attitude almost guarantees that no one will take you seriously. Communication in writing is like any human relationship: Nothing important or interesting happens unless you really care.

To put reading with care in perspective, let's first look at three popular approaches to revising, editing, and proofreading—approaches guaranteed not to work.

HOW NOT TO REVISE: EPISODE 1

You greet the morning with surly indifference and a yawn. You were up late last night, drafting a paper, and your face now feels puffy and tired, the result of roughing out some tentative ideas. Your mouth tastes like a battlefield for tiny creatures of unknown origin.

You lean toward tattered pages.

Familiar words beckon.

And then you begin.

You're exhausted, so it's tough to concentrate—to read your draft from someone else's perspective. Instead, your eyes caress each phrase in passing. Because you're tired, you see your words as separate jewels—each shimmering and precious, stunningly profound. Each, after all, expresses the spiritual essence of you, the insightful writer.

You close your eyes, thinking about the night before. In quest of words and sentences, you made a journey to hell and back again. These are words fashioned of pain and suffering, and you are not about to change them now. To rethink or reorganize your text demands more energy than you can muster. You can't distance yourself from this writing.

Tinkering is dangerous, you tell yourself. Better leave well enough alone. The "raw energy" of your prose will surely count for something once it's typed up.

This frees you to keep a cafeteria date.

 HOW NOT TO EDIT: EPISODE 2

It's afternoon now, and your paper is due tomorrow. Your writing instructor has asked you to hand in your rough draft along with the final copy. Although you didn't make any real revisions earlier in the day, you now feel a need to make some editing changes just for the sake of appearances.

You lay out your rough draft.

You open your thesaurus.

And then you begin.

You're reading sentence by sentence, looking for simple words that you might replace with longer, more ponderous ones. You find a number of such words and sprinkle them like plump raisins in yeasty dough. The organizational problems, logical gaps, and lack of development are still there in your prose, but the bigger words seem to dress up the page.

Reading through your text one last time, you realize that you can also make the sentences fancier by lengthening them. You begin adding modifiers and qualifiers, trying to make your writing sound like a highly academic treatise. You also slip in a few folksy clichés to give your prose added zing. You punctuate and capitalize in creative ways.

That should do it, you tell yourself. Putting in extra padding certainly makes your writing impressive—a "fun lesson" in elegant vocabulary for your reader.

This frees you for the mindlessness of final typing.

HOW NOT TO PROOFREAD: EPISODE 3

It's early evening now, and you're hungry. The typed pages of your final paper—much the same as last night's draft—lie scattered before you. It's time to put your text in final shape, you tell yourself—time for a once-over-lightly proofreading, the last step of prose surgery before supper.

Words swim before your eyes.

You glance at your watch.

And then you begin.

You're reading at your normal rate—say, 200 to 250 words per minute—or maybe a little faster because you're eager to "put your writing to bed," as journalists say. It's easy to cruise; after all, you already know what the message is. You zip down one page and then another. You're on automatic pilot, detached from the text.

Because of your high-speed reading, you are filling in words and meanings where none exists. You are reading from memory, not noticing the misspelled words, dropped endings, and missing punctuation. You pause as you finish your charade of proofreading. The text is a mine field of errors, but you've made your way through unscathed.

Not too bad, you think to yourself. Now that it's typed into final form, it seems to make sense. After all, a good appearance is half the battle in writing.

This frees you to indulge in self-congratulation.

Do any of these episodes sound familiar? If so, the chances are that you've never learned—or really practiced—the kind of reading essential for prose surgery.

If you care about the quality of your work, you must realize that writing well is a tricky process—sometimes consisting of one step forward and two steps back. Within you is an endless stream of words that can replace or modify the ones on the page; but you have to budget plenty of time for real revising and editing, not just a few minutes for recopying your work.

Another point to remember is that readers have only your words to go by—nothing else. So to revise well, you have to read from another's point of view. By "becoming" your intended audience, you make changes based on what feels right for your text, not for your ego. As noted earlier, this process consists of listening carefully to your text to hear what needs to be said—then listening again. It takes practice.

BECOMING ANOTHER READER

In your schooling so far, instructors have probably emphasized the value of speed reading for covering material. But the reading required to become another reader is much *slower* than normal. It's not unusual to spend several minutes tinkering with a sentence or two.

Some writers whisper their words to themselves; others actually read aloud. But whatever their approach, they tend to cover the same ground over and over, hearing how words, phrases, and sentences connect.

As you learn to read with care, you also learn to consider factors *beyond* your words—for example, questions or objections that a reader might have. In other words, you learn to "doubt" your own writing, to ask yourself, Does this make sense? What supports this position? Where does this conclusion come from? Why this sequence of points? You become a devil's advocate, inviting yourself to think more deeply about what you've written.

Finally, as you read carefully and systematically, your emphasis shifts. That is, in one reading you focus on the development of ideas, in another on style. Because of these shifts in focus, each reading helps you think about your text in a different way.

Entering the consciousness of someone else—a special kind of reader—means shifting your reading attitude as well as your reading method. The principles of this shift, to repeat, are these: (1) reading slowly, (2) whispering to yourself or reading aloud, (3) "doubting" your own writing, and (4) reading for different purposes. Let's consider each point in a little more detail.

1. *Reading slowly.* To slow down your reading, you may find it helpful at first to use a simple pacer—a 5 by 8 card. Move the pacer down the page to reveal your words gradually rather than all at once. By curbing your regular rush-ahead reading habits, this technique enables you to see the words of your text in a fresh way.

Put another way, the pacer card helps to focus your attention. Such focus is essential for slow, deliberate reading. After achieving focus, you also need to think, What is this saying? Does it really make sense? Where's the main point here? How does this idea logically follow? Focus helps you become a different reader, one who is reading your ideas for the first time. Your words become this reader's lifeline.

2. *Whispering to yourself or reading aloud.* People who write professionally always advise students to read aloud.

Only by actually hearing your prose, they say, can you tell whether it works. For example, this sentence would not pass a read-aloud test:

> Learning skills is important.

Two meanings are possible: (1) the learning of skills is important, and (2) the skills of learning are important. Even if the intended meaning is the first one, the read-aloud test points to a need for prose surgery.

Moreover, if you read aloud and hear yourself pause at specific points in a sentence, as you are now doing, you know that you probably need punctuation. On the other hand, if your writing is studded with punctuation marks that have no effect on oral reading, you probably need to make some changes. Reading aloud helps to connect your speaking and writing voices. There's no substitute for it.

"Doubting" your own writing. Each of us has within us an intelligent **best self,** a self who sorts through sense and nonsense. This best self is the person you should write to please. And it is this person's "doubting" questions that you should try to answer.

For example, your best self may read your prose and pause repeatedly at a particular sentence, frowning slightly. This is important feedback. It tells you that something is wrong. Or your best self may murmur something in your inner ear about a flat opening or say "yes, but" to one of your examples. Or your best self may cock an eyebrow at a sentence like this one:

> Correct spelling, accurate punctuation, standard usage—these are the basic tools on which a foundation of meaning can be built.

A "foundation built on tools"? What? Your best self will not let such a sentence go unrevised and unedited.

Reading for different purposes. After disciplining yourself to be attentive, to whisper, and to "doubt" your own prose, concentrate on reading purposefully. While editing, for example, you might focus your first reading on sentence structure and usage. A second reading might focus on punctuation and capitalization, particularly if these are problems for you. Your third reading might focus on spelling, checking words that you're uncertain about or that have given you trouble in the past.

Such readings are somewhat like a pilot's checklist. Pilots know that they can greatly reduce their chances for error by proceeding systematically through a complex process. The key is to pay attention as each subsystem is checked out—and then double-check to make sure that no system has been overlooked. As noted earlier, to focus on one thing at a time is to work smarter, not harder.

In summary, the imaginative leap of becoming another reader does not happen overnight. It takes work. But the more you pay attention to meaning—practicing the basic skills described above—the more your best self will nod approval.

PROSE SURGERY IN PERSPECTIVE

To help you learn the skills of prose surgery, your instructor may use a workshop approach to writing. This approach typically involves you in peer response groups—usually three to five students—and in brief conferences with your instructor. When you are working with other students, your paper is called a response draft; when you are working with your instructor, your paper is called a conference draft. This terminology will be used throughout the book. The purpose of a workshop approach is to provide useful feedback for your drafting, revising, and editing efforts.

By listening to the comments of your peers and instructor—and by asking them questions—you can learn much about how to revise and edit. Of course, learning from others requires openness on your part. If you are defensive or argumentative about your writing and deny the validity of others' comments and suggestions, you will cut off the possibility of improving or clarifying your text.

Certain comments from your peers and instructor will probably *confirm* your hunches about strengths or weaknesses in your writing, while others will *challenge* you to rethink the content, organization, or style of your text. After listening to feedback from others, you will no doubt act upon certain suggestions but ignore others. Your intentions as a writer govern such decisions about revising and editing. Remember: No one can make these decisions for you.

The process of getting and giving feedback about writing in progress requires your commitment. You will be asked to read others' work with care and to verbalize your responses. Of course, the more specific you can make your responses and questions, the better. Here are some simple guidelines for getting and giving feedback.

How to Get Feedback on Writing

1. Read your work aloud twice.

2. Don't "defend" your work.

3. Take notes on what others tell you.

4. Ask questions to clarify what others say.

5. Thank people for their comments.

6. Never apologize for the piece you're going to read.

How to Give Feedback on Writing

1. Listen for the overall effect in the first reading.

2. Make notes/comments during the second reading.

3. Tell what you liked best about the writing.

4. Identify a place in the writing that may need work.

5. Comment on content and organization first, then mechanics.

6. Be specific by "pointing" to places on the actual page.

To facilitate a collaborative give-and-take, you should make photocopies of your draft so that others can *see* your text as you read it aloud; your peers will do the same for their writing. After a response-group session, you should receive back your photocopied drafts so that you can revise and edit on your own.

In this connection, editor Maxwell Perkins is said to have once remarked, "Just get it down on paper, and then we'll see what to do with it." Such advice is worth remembering as you begin to study revising and editing. You don't have to get everything "right" in a first and final draft. All you have to do is get it down. It's with the support of your peers and instructor that your "best self," who serves as editor, can take over.

You and your peers will probably find the following shorthand a helpful one for making marginal notations; your instructor may also use this same system for commenting on your early drafts:

Responding to Writing

Make marginal notes, using these four symbols. Then give constructive feedback to the writer.

+ = I like this [word, phrase, sentence].

√ = Please check this [word, phrase, sentence].

? = I don't follow this [word, phrase, sentence].

= Think about developing this part more.

In each of this book's six chapters on revising and editing, you will see how my students and I have used this marking system. Look for the feature called "Prose Surgery in Action."

This notation system enables you to comment at the level of the word, phrase, or sentence. You can put these marks either in the margin or at particular places within the text that deserve comment; also, you can underline sentences or bracket certain paragraphs and use these marks as a way of commenting. In your follow-up conversations, you will then have specific places in the text to refer to. Also, these notes will serve as reminders as you revise and edit.

The best prose surgeons know that the text itself is a far richer source of information than any set of admonitions or arbitrary rules. Prose surgeons take their time, paying attention to the voice of the writing as well as its silences. Their aim, always, is to read with a "listening eye"—to hear what the writing says and doesn't say. They treat the text with care and respect. In this way, they encourage the words themselves to reveal what they need in the way of help.

Exercises in this book will help you learn the basics of prose surgery; but, obviously, exercises are not your own writing. As a prose surgeon intern, then, it's your job to apply what you learn to your own work in progress. Be active in your learning. Make the exercises work *for* you. It's a basic principle of learning that whatever tasks you can do with help, you can eventually do on your own.

An old proverb says that "surgeons cut that they may cure." When your rough drafts begin to open up to you— almost to diagnose themselves—you'll know that you've arrived as a prose surgeon. In the meantime, have fun with *Writing Incisively.*

READING TO REVISE: WRITING MORE FULLY

> *"Hack" surgeons only give "cutting" advice, but surgeons who care take time for "patient" interaction.*
>
> —YOUR INSTRUCTOR

Scene: An office conference with your writing instructor.

"You've made a start in your paper," your instructor says. "But—I don't know quite how to put this—"

"It's undeveloped," you fill in. "Thin. Needs examples to support the generalizations. Needs more detail."

Your instructor nods. "You took the words right out of my mouth."

"I've heard it all before," you reply. "I know what the problem is. I just don't know what to do about it."

"Maybe your writing needs to answer certain questions."

"Questions?" you ask.

"The reader's questions. After all, 'undeveloped' is just a quick way of saying that the reader has unanswered questions."

You think about this for a moment.

"You see, writing is a conversation," your instructor continues. "And in most conversations there are questions. Just a moment ago, for example, you asked a question when something wasn't clear."

"Okay, sure."

"And just now your nod told me you're getting what I'm saying. It's feedback to me, the speaker."

"So what does this have to do with writing?" you ask.

Your instructor pauses. "Just this: In this conversation, I can *hear* your questions. And I can sense by watching your reactions whether we're communicating. But things are different in writing. I can't see your frowns or nods. I have to anticipate your reactions to what I've written."

"Uh, say that again?"

"I have to *imagine* the questions that you as a reader probably have. In other words, I try to guess, from the flow of the text itself, whether you're likely to get it."

"You mean because there's no feedback."

"Right. When you're writing, you have to become both speaker *and* listener. And the listener's job is to create questions that the speaker tries to answer."

"So I need to ask more questions?"

"Exactly. Read between the lines of your text. And as you do, ask the questions that you, as an intelligent listener, would ask of the speaker."

"For example?"

"That's always a good one," your instructor says, handing back your paper. "Try it on some of your sentences."

CHAPTER PREVIEW

In this book's introduction, you learned about the importance of reading with care and "becoming another reader" as you revise. This chapter deals with the constructive part of prose surgery—namely, adding details to support underdeveloped prose. You'll learn how to use questions as a basic tool when doing this revising.

The scenario above suggests that writing is like a conversation in which you're both speaker and listener. Adding material enables you to answer questions that your reader is likely to have. By asking (and answering) these questions, you create direction for revision. And you therefore write more fully, not to mention more incisively.

This chapter will introduce you to a variety of sentence starters, which help to create sentence variety. Toward the end of the chapter, you'll focus on various transitions and the hidden questions that underlie them. These transitions will be especially useful as you begin revising your own writing in progress.

Take your time when adding details and support; ask thoughtful questions. Check the built-in answers *after* completing the exercises, not before. To maximize your learning, make sure to compare your revision practice with that done by other students.

EXPANDING, NOT PADDING

Adding details and support to undeveloped prose enables you to expand your paragraphs and thereby write more fully. But *expanding* is not *padding*. As a prose surgeon, your aim is to enhance natural lines of development, not to create puffy bulges.

To illustrate the process of adding details and support, let's first consider a bare, undeveloped paragraph that is part of a brief character sketch. Here, as elsewhere in this book, we'll *list* individual sentences in the paragraph so that they're easy to study. Later in this chapter, we'll work with other paragraphs on **procrastination,** the fine art of putting things off until tomorrow.

Procrastination

As the deadline approaches, Max glances at his watch.

His blood pressure rises with his anger.

Max has procrastinated for weeks on his project.

This is not his first flirtation with disaster.

For Max, procrastination is no laughing matter.

While the preceding paragraph might be useful for some purposes, it fails to answer a number of questions that a reader might have, among them:

How is Max's tension revealed?

How does he look?

What has he done to procrastinate?

How has he procrastinated in the past?

Why is his procrastination so serious?

By combining the basic paragraph with a reader's questions, we can generate more material and more reader interest. Let's try interspersing the reader questions with the original sentences.

As the deadline approaches, Max glances at his watch.
How is Max's tension revealed?

His blood pressure rises with his anger.
How does he look?

Max has procrastinated for weeks on his project.
What has he done to procrastinate?

This is not his first flirtation with disaster.
How has he procrastinated in the past?

For Max, procrastination is no laughing matter.
Why is his procrastination so serious?

Each of the questions could generate several sentences of response; and these sentences, in turn, could generate *more* questions. As you can see, asking questions as a reader is a powerful yet easy-to-use revision strategy for adding details and support to your writing. Here's a brief paragraph built upon the five preceding questions.

As the deadline approaches, Max glances at his watch.

He grits his teeth, trying to pull together what he knows will be a weak, sloppy report.

His blood pressure rises with his anger.

Tiny beads of sweat appear along his forehead as he searches without success for missing information.

Max has procrastinated for weeks on his project.

Among other excuses, he has told himself that he needs a large block of uninterrupted time.

This is not his first flirtation with disaster.

In fact, he has now acquired a reputation for undependability.

For Max, procrastination is no laughing matter.

It now threatens his job security.

Notice how this paragraph holds more interest than the earlier one. Why is this? Because it has some depth of detail. Each answer to a question adds detail, which in turn adds interest. In this chapter, you'll learn how to do this reconstructive work on your own.

ANSWERING YOUR READER'S QUESTIONS

In answering your reader's questions, you write down what makes sense in the context of emerging paragraphs. By practicing this process in the Do-It-Yourself exercises that follow, you'll see the potential of adding details and support in your own writing.

Notice in the next exercise that three sentence starters follow each question. Select one of these or make up your

own. Then answer the given question in a way that seems
to "fit" the emerging paragraph.

EXERCISE 1.1: PROCRASTINATION
(Adding Details and Support)

Procrastination is not a physical problem.

So what kind of problem is it?

1. It results instead . . .

2. Rather, it stems from . . .

3. According to the dictionary, it . . .

EXPANSION _____

_____

_____

The effects of procrastination surround us.

What are they?

1. They include . . .

2. Among them are . . .

3. Tardiness, late work . . .

EXPANSION _____

_____

_____

In fact, just about everybody procrastinates at one time or
another.

Why do we do this?

1. We do this because . . .

2. We procrastinate so that . . .

3. The reason for this is that . . .

EXPANSION _____

_____

_____

Procrastination becomes a problem when it becomes habitual.

What would be an example?

1. The person who . . .

2. For example, the . . .

3. An illustration would be . . .

EXPANSION _____

_____

_____

In short, procrastination is a self-defeating behavior.

What does it do?

1. It prevents . . .

2. It keeps a person from . . .

3. It undermines a person's . . .

EXPANSION _____

_____

_____

Did you notice how sentence starters emerged directly from underlying questions? Did you notice, too, how each starter pointed your follow-up answer in a slightly different direction?

Actually, the form of sentence starters helps make a transition between existing sentences and ones you're adding for details and support. You'll study starters and transitions in more detail later in this chapter. For now, simply note that different sentence starters help you achieve sentence variety in your revision work.

There are, of course, many possibilities for expanding the preceding sentences. Check with other students in your class and share your sentences with them. Just for the record, here's one paragraph to compare with yours.

Procrastination is not a physical problem.

Instead, it stems from an individual's psychological state—sometimes from feelings of low self-esteem.

The effects of procrastination surround us.

They include unanswered letters, unpaid bills, unfixed faucets, and lots of other good intentions followed by broken promises.

In fact, just about everybody procrastinates at one time or another.

We do it in order to put off what we regard as unpleasant tasks—getting up at dawn, mowing the grass, going on a diet.

Procrastination becomes a problem when it becomes habitual.

For example, many students and teachers are notorious for putting off their writing assignments and paper correction until the last possible minute—and sometimes beyond.

In short, procrastination is a self-defeating behavior.

It creates tension and guilt within the individual and sometimes has serious real-world consequences.

CREATING QUESTIONS FOR EXPANSION

So far you've seen how to answer a reader's potential questions. Now let's turn to the questions themselves—first asking them, then thinking about answers. In other words, let's pull together the process of adding details and support.

In actual revision, it's unlikely that you'd question *every* sentence in your text and then compose answers. Here the process is extended to show what goes on "beneath the surface" as you become a thoughtful reader and look back at an underdeveloped draft. Questioning and composing may occur almost simultaneously in real revising—as a single act of mind, not as separate steps.

To illustrate question asking in revision, let's consider how we might deal with this sentence:

Many procrastinators are perfectionists in disguise.

As intelligent readers, we might ask, So what? What does this mean? Why is this? We might ask other questions as well—for example, Who says so? What are the disguises of procrastinators?

The "best" question depends on your *aims* as a writer. You can't answer all questions, so you choose one that fits your intentions and the paragraph context. This point is crucial. By putting yourself in the reader's shoes, asking mental questions, and choosing one to answer, you set your own agenda for revision.

Read the first statement in the following exercise. Then choose one question from above—or create another—to follow it. With that done, create a single question to follow each statement in the rest of the exercise. For now, *don't answer the questions that you pose;* you'll do that later.

EXERCISE 1.2: PROCRASTINATION
(Adding Details and Support)

Many procrastinators are perfectionists in disguise.

QUESTION _____

EXPANSION _____

_____

But perfectionism is an attitude that procrastinators can change.

QUESTION _____

EXPANSION _____

_____

A job doesn't have to be done perfectly.

QUESTION _____

EXPANSION _____

_____

Procrastinators should "think small" as they face a task.

QUESTION _____

EXPANSION _____

_____

Procrastinators should also organize time into chunks ranging from fifteen to thirty minutes.

QUESTION _____

EXPANSION _____

_____

_____

As a reward for accomplishments, the procrastinator needs to look back frequently.

QUESTION _____

EXPANSION _____

_____

The preceding exercise in question asking isn't easy. Here, after all, you're beginning to explore revision as a complex thinking process, not merely as a write-by-numbers mechanical skill.

Now, compare the questions you asked with those that follow. Proceeding question by question, put a check mark (√) next to your question each time you see it as more interesting than the corresponding one below. Make changes in your questions as they occur to you. Please be prepared to discuss in class why your final questions might be interesting to a reader.

What does "perfectionists in disguise" mean?

Why is recognition of this fact important?

What has to happen instead of "perfection"?

What is an example of "thinking small"?

Why should procrastinators organize time into small chunks?

What is the effect of looking back frequently?

When your questions are in final written form, return to Exercise 1.2. Your task now is to answer the questions in the form of "expansion" sentences. Take your time, adding details and support.

After writing out these sentences, read through your completed paragraph, omitting the questions. Then read through the paragraph below. Whenever you prefer your own expansion sentence to one shown here, give yourself a check mark (√). Also, be ready to compare your sentences with those of other students. By examining their questions and answers, you'll see new ways to add details and support.

Many procrastinators are perfectionists in disguise.

In other words, they believe that only with more time can they do a job "right."

But perfectionism is an attitude that procrastinators can change.

They need to realize that unrealistic standards of performance create problems with self-esteem.

A job doesn't have to be done perfectly.

Instead, it just needs to be dealt with in a timely manner.

Procrastinators should "think small" as they face a task.

For example, they might first plan how to approach the task and create a timetable for its completion.

Procrastinators should also organize time into chunks ranging from fifteen to thirty minutes.

Accomplishing small parts of a larger task creates momentum for the procrastinator—the feeling of being in control.

As a reward for accomplishments, the procrastinator needs to look back frequently.

These reviews help the procrastinator to see the total task in perspective and to feel encouraged by success.

MORE ON ANSWERING QUESTIONS

Earlier in this chapter you saw how sentence starters could point your expanion sentences in different directions. They provide transitions between sentences as well as sentence variety.

Let's focus on creating sentence starters during revision. Consider, for example, this statement and a possible follow-up question:

Clearly, procrastination is a complex behavior pattern.
So what?

To answer this question, you might point out that understanding a behavior pattern helps us to deal with it—that knowledge gives us power. Various sentence starters could be used to express this idea. Here are just a few:

1. Equally clear is the fact that . . .

2. Its complexity must be understood so that . . .

3. However, in order to deal with it effectively . . .

Being able to express an idea in several ways gives you options for adding details and support. Once again, *you set the direction for revision.*

Read through the following exercise, and think of possible answers to the questions posed. Hold these answers in mind. Sentence starters have been created for the first statement. Create sentence starters for each of the following statements, keeping your answers in mind.

For now, *don't write out the expansion sentences;* you'll do that later. Take your time with this revision activity. *Remember:* There are many "right" answers.

EXERCISE 1.3: PROCRASTINATION
(Adding Details and Support)

Clearly, procrastination is a complex behavior pattern.

So what?

1. Equally clear is the fact that . . .

2. Its complexity must be understood so that . . .

3. However, in order to deal with it effectively . . .

EXPANSION _____

_____

_____

The roots of procrastination lie within one's self-concept.

Can you put this another way?

1. _____

2. _____

3. _____

EXPANSION _____

_____

_____

According to many psychologists, procrastination is caused by a fear of failure.

What does fear of failure result from?

1. _____

2. _____

3. _____

EXPANSION _____

_____

_____

As noted earlier, procrastinators are often perfectionists at heart.

So what?

1. _____

2. _____

3. _____

EXPANSION _____

_____

_____

Procrastination thus becomes a psychological cop-out.

How can this point be explained?

1. _____

2. _____

3. _____

EXPANSION _____

_____

_____

The procrastinator tries to blame circumstances for delays.

What is the truth of the matter?

1. _____

2. _____

3. _____

EXPANSION

Now, compare your sentence starters with those that follow. If you prefer yours, put a check mark (√) next to it. If you prefer one of the following to yours, put a check mark next to it. As you do this activity, notice how different starters create different directions for revision. Please be prepared to discuss your choices in class.

Can you put this another way?

1. That is . . .

2. More simply . . .

3. In other words . . .

What does fear of failure result from?

1. This fear results from . . .

2. Fear of failure is the result of . . .

3. Resulting from low self-esteem, this . . .

So what?

1. In order to avoid facing . . .

2. Procrastinators delay so that . . .

3. Unable to meet their own standards . . .

How can this point be explained?

1. It amounts to . . .

2. It is really a way of . . .

3. It enables the individual to . . .

What is the truth of the matter?

1. But such excuses . . .

2. And yet circumstances are . . .

3. However, the real responsibility . . .

So far, so good. Your task now is to write out expansion sentences for Exercise 1.3. After choosing the sentence starters you like, write sentences that fit the emerging context of the paragraph. As before, take your time with this activity. Do your best to add details and support.

Compare your expansion sentences with the ones that follow. As you check (√) the sentences you prefer, remember that this activity has no "right answers." Your sentences can be quite different from these and still be highly effective. In class, compare your expansion sentences with those of other students. Such comparisons will help you learn more about how to add details and support.

Clearly, procrastination is a complex behavior pattern.

To understand it more fully, however, is to gain some power over it.

The roots of procrastination lie within one's self-concept.

More simply, procrastinators view themselves negatively and have doubts about their self-worth.

According to many psychologists, procrastination is caused by a fear of failure.

This fear results from low self-esteem.

As noted earlier, procrastinators are often perfectionists at heart.

Unable to meet their own standards, procrastinators delay to avoid facing those standards.

Procrastination thus becomes a psychological cop-out.

It enables the individual to avoid facing the root of his or her problems.

The procrastinator tries to blame circumstances for delays.

But such excuses are merely the procrastinator's way of avoiding personal responsibility.

USING TRANSITIONS

In this chapter we've procrastinated enough. Let's now consider how transitional words and phrases provide starters for answers to various questions. The following list of transition categories, presented alphabetically, can help you add details and support to prose that explains or persuades.

Each transitional word or phrase serves as a signpost for your reader. This is, it signals the kind of question that is going to be answered. Take time to study the transition categories and questions. Then look at the words and phrases that serve as signposts. To learn how these transitional words and phrases work in context, read back through some of the expanded procrastination paragraphs in this chapter. You'll spot many of them.

As you read through a draft of your own writing later, open the book to these pages. Find a section of your text that needs details and support. Scanning down the questions below, you'll see how certain questions "fit" immediately. The appropriate sentence starters (transitions, in this case) are at your fingertips.

Addition: *What more can be added?*

also, and, again, besides, furthermore, in addition, moreover, not only . . . but also, too

Concession: *Is there another viewpoint?*

admittedly, certainly, granted, no doubt, obviously, of course, to be sure

Conclusion: *What is the summary or conclusion?*

finally, in brief, in closing (conclusion), in summary, lastly, then, to conclude, to sum up (summarize)

Consequence: *What is the effect or result?*

accordingly, and so, consequently, for this reason, hence, so, therefore, then, thus

Contrast: *What are the points of difference?*

actually, at the same time, but, conversely, however, in contrast, instead, nevertheless, on the contrary, on the other hand, rather, still, yet

Likeness: *What are the points of similarity?*

by (in) comparison, by the same token, in like manner, in similiar fashion, likewise, similarly

Example: *What are examples or illustrations?*

as an example (illustration), by way of example (illustration), for example (instance), say, to take a case in point

Restatement: *How can the point be put another way?*

in brief, indeed, in fact, in short, more simply, namely, put another way, specifically, that is, in other words

Sequence: *In what order do the points occur?*

finally; first/second/third, and so on; for one thing/for another (thing); last; the former/the latter

Time: *In what order do the events occur?*

afterward, at the same time, before, earlier, formerly, later on, meanwhile, now, simultaneously, subsequently

Of course, not all expansion questions are phrased as these are; but watch for questions such as these in your expansion work. Also, refer to this list of transitions periodically to keep them in mind. By paying attention to these words and phrases in your outside reading, you'll see how they create "connectedness" in prose.

LOOKING BACK, LOOKING AHEAD

This chapter on adding details and support has focused on the revision skill of asking and answering questions as well as creating sentence starters and transitions. We noted that this process happens rapidly during actual revision but that it has been slowed down here to help you understand how it is done, step by step.

Four follow-up exercises provide opportunities for you to practice skills you've learned in this chapter. Then in Exercise 1.8 you'll apply question asking and answering to your own writing. Applying the strategy will help make it part of your revision habits and contribute to your success as a prose surgeon. Having learned *how*, you should give it a try.

Chapter 2 builds upon what you've just learned. You'll study a fundamental principle of writing—levels of generality—and learn two basic frameworks for paragraph development—coordinate and subordinate sequence. You'll also see how to reorganize sentences for clarity and to delete sentences (and paragraphs) that don't support your aims.

 ## DO-IT-YOURSELF EXERCISES

Please be prepared to share your work in class. Your instructor will provide suggested answers for Exercises 1.4–1.7. Use Exercise 1.8 to make a personal application of adding details and support.

EXERCISE 1.4: SLY
(Adding Details and Support)

Sly was hardly a handsome man.

What was his general appearance?

1. He was pale . . .

2. He looked awkward . . .

3. Heavyset and disheveled . . .

EXPANSION _____

_____

His black eyes were close-set and unusually small.

What else was distinctive about his eyes?

1. They gleamed . . .

2. They shifted back . . .

3. Their lack of emotion . . .

EXPANSION _____

_____

He sported a narrow pencil-line mustache.

What effect did the mustache have?

1. It looked . . .

2. Its severity . . .

3. It made him appear . . .

EXPANSION _____

_____

His dark hair glistened from the sweet, oily cream he used on it.

What did his hair look like (or suggest)?

1. It gleamed like . . .

2. Its scent suggested . . .

3. Combed straight back, it . . .

EXPANSION _____

_____

Sly was not the kind of man you regarded as a friend.

What kind of man was he?

1. He was . . .

2. Rather, . . .

3. Instead, . . .

EXPANSION _____

_____

EXERCISE 1.5: PLAYOFF SHOT
(Adding Details and Support)

Just before the final buzzer, the crowd went wild.

Why?

EXPANSION _____

_____

Cheryl muscled down a crucial rebound in the opponent's court.

What did the other players do?

EXPANSION _____

_____

With time running out, she dribbled down the sidelines toward her team's basket.

What was the crowd's reaction?

EXPANSION _____

_____

As a teammate broke into the clear, Cheryl flicked her the ball.

How did her teammate react?

EXPANSION _____

_____

Now unguarded, Cheryl looped behind the defenders and took her teammate's return pass.

What was her next move?

EXPANSION _____

_____

She released her shot with a soft touch, banking it against the glass.

What happened then?

EXPANSION _____

_____

EXERCISE 1.6: WRITER'S BLOCK
(Adding Details and Support)

There are times when I have nothing to say.

Describe how your mind feels.

EXPANSION _____

_____

This emptiness reveals itself in my appearance.

How do you appear?

EXPANSION _____

_____

I search for words on a wordless horizon.

What do you listen for?

EXPANSION _____

_____

But all of these efforts are in vain.

Why are they in vain?

EXPANSION _____

_____

Finally, in frustration, I give in to silence.

What does the silence do?

EXPANSION _____

_____

It is out of this silence that something begins to happen on its own.

What happens?

EXPANSION _____

_____

These first words are like rain after a long dry spell.

How do they feel?

EXPANSION _____

_____

EXERCISE 1.7: OLD PEOPLE
(Adding Details and Support)

Many societies respect and honor the experience of old people, but ours does not.

QUESTION _____

EXPANSION _____

_____

This national attitude demeans our senior citizens.

QUESTION _____

EXPANSION _____

_____

However, the elderly could help our nation address the issue of child care for working mothers.

QUESTION _____

EXPANSION _____

_____

Many old people would willingly provide the love and care that these children need.

QUESTION _____

EXPANSION _____

_____

Yet children are shuttled off to day-care centers that are often little more than warehouses for the young.

QUESTION _____

EXPANSION _____

_____

But "efficiency" is the name of the game, and children receive little individual attention.

QUESTION _____

EXPANSION _____

_____

In short, the elderly often have time to love those who need it.

QUESTION _____

EXPANSION _____

_____

EXERCISE 1.8: PERSONAL APPLICATION

Select a draft of your writing in progress, or find a paper you've written that needs further development. Read through the paper carefully; identify a section that might be improved by added details and support. You'll need at least fifteen to twenty sentences for this revision activity.

Make a photocopy of the section you intend to revise. Put a number after each sentence in the section. Now, on a separate sheet of paper, list the numbers of these sentences like this:

1. Q:
   A:

2. Q:
   A:

3. Q:
   A:

You're now ready to engage in the question asking and answering process you practiced earlier in this chapter. Reread your problem section, sentence by sentence. Wherever you see a place to ask an important question, do so. Write down your questions (and their corresponding answers) on the sheet you've prepared, next to the appropriate number. *Note:* You don't have to ask questions after *all* of your sentences.

To make a revised text, recopy all of your original sentences, along with their numbers. Add details and support from your numbered answers at the appropriate places. Reread your revised writing. Ask yourself, Is the revised text stronger and more interesting than the original? In what specific ways? What have I learned about revision from this activity? Write up your answers to these questions in as much detail as possible.

Hand in your work from this application activity. Your packet of materials should contain the following: (1) a photocopy of your original rough draft, (2) a page of questions and answers keyed by number to sentences in your draft, (3) your revised text (recopied original sentences plus added details and support), and (4) a summary statement evaluating the two pieces of text and what you learned about revision.

 **PROSE SURGERY IN ACTION**

Powerful and vivid life experiences make indelible impressions on us; but sometimes what is clear to us personally—because we've *lived* the experience—is not clear to our readers. To write incisively, we must put ourselves in the reader's shoes—must read the *writing*, not our remembered experiences.

Trent Rasmussen learned this when he began to revise and edit a personal essay. When others read the first paragraph of his response draft and said they didn't understand what was happening—who "he" was in the first sentence—Trent was puzzled. He had *lived* the event, so it was clear to him. When someone noted that "him" in the second and third sentences could refer either to Scott or to the mysterious "he," Trent began to see the problem. Readers needed more background if they were to read with understanding.

As Trent questioned his own writing, he began to see a need to be more explicit, to add details and support. Notice how his conference draft clarifies most of the pronoun problems. After his conference, Trent realized that he could do still more. He questioned his draft further and wrote a new opening that put the reader in a physical place, the setting for his essay. Note, too, how he put background information in the *middle* of his paper (the fifth paragraph), not at the beginning.

Here are the four symbols used in class and in conferences to prompt revision and editing:

+ = I like this [word, phrase, sentence].
√ = Please check this [word, phrase, sentence].
? = I don't follow this [word, phrase, sentence].
= Think about developing this part more.

Practice Doesn't Always Make Perfect
(Response Draft)

Gesturing with a calculated jerk of his head, Scott whispered,
"He'll be coming out right over there." I stretched my neck
toward him as I tried to make out his statement and acknowl- *who?*
edged by a barely noticeable nod. Signalling him to be quiet *+ action*
by bringing a finger to my lips, I crouched lower, wanting
desperately to make myself invisible. I watched Scott as he
did likewise a few yards to my left.

[*This draft goes on to describe a personal experience.*]

Practice Doesn't Always Make Perfect
(Conference Draft)

I stretched my neck toward Scott as I tried to make out his
whispered statement. Gesturing with a calculated jerk of his
head, he whispered, "He'll be coming out right over there." I
acknowledged *with* by a barely noticeable nod. Signalling him to *British*
be quiet by bringing a finger to my lips, I crouched lower, *sp.*
wanting desperately to make myself invisible. I watched Scott
as he did likewise a few yards to my left. In the dim morning
light his camoflage helped him disappear among the trees. *# show*
                                                              setting
[There was no more sound from the forest as I could hear *# show*
                                                          emotion
nothing over the uncontrolled pounding of my heart. It seemed
as if I was destined to die of cardiac arrest at seventeen. Swal-

lowing hard, I realized my hands were shaking. My adrenalin was pushing my self-control to its limit.

[*This draft goes on to describe a personal experience.*]

Practice Doesn't Always Make Perfect
by
Trent Rasmussen

The snapping of a distant twig jolted me back to reality. "You hear that?" I whispered to my brother Scott. He nodded and gestured toward the dark pines that loomed in front of us. Signaling him to be quiet by bringing a finger to my lips, I crouched lower, wanting desperately to melt into the shadows. I watched as Scott did likewise a few yards to my left. He glanced at me over his shoulder. His eyes were alive with excitement. Or was it fear?

An early snow had already painted the higher mountains white and reminded us that winter would soon replace this beautiful autumn season. The morning air was cold, but not uncomfortable, and the pink flow over the eastern slopes promised that the sun would soon splash its warmth over us. Small patches of mist hovering near the ground created an eerie atmosphere, and the silence of the forest added to my temporary uneasiness.

I squinted as I scanned the wall of pine trees in front of us. The frosted grass of the clearing provided a harsh contrast to the dark pines that grew on the other side. Scattered quaking aspen created explosions of golden color among the shadows of the pines.

Movement up the hill caught my eye, and as I turned my head to afford a better view, the largest elk I had ever seen materialized out of the mist. His sudden appearance had caught me off guard. As he moved out of the shadows, a silent sigh escaped my lips. He was huge! My breathing became a series of short gasps; I heard nothing over the uncontrolled pounding of my heart. Swallowing hard, I felt my hands shaking. Adrenalin was pushing my self-control to the limit.

I had practiced all summer with my bow in order to be ready when an opportunity such as this presented itself. Hour after hour Scott and I would shoot arrows into our straw-bale targets, all the while imagining ourselves stalking the forest as though we were supermen of the archer world. We would fight off the boredom of practice by reminding ourselves that someday our diligence would be rewarded.

The long hours of monotonous practice and sore muscles were far from my mind now. At this point, I knew that my reflexes would take over. I could do this in my sleep. One quick, last look over my equipment assured me that all was in order.

As I watched the elk move gracefully along his chosen path, my eyes were riveted on his antlers. The quick calculations racing through my mind convinced me that I was looking at the largest elk of all time. The elk continued to close the gap between us, oblivious to the two camouflaged bodies lying in wait. He grew larger all the time. His antlers stretched up and back as though they had no end. How could he carry them and not topple over? He moved across the clearing silently, with all the elegance and grace of a ballroom dancer. He walked deliberately, stopping only once as his body tensed and he tested the air for danger. Satisfied that all was safe, he moved on. He looked close enough to touch. Then, as though he had been a ghost, the elk disappeared into the shadows as silently and unceremoniously as he had appeared.

As my heart rate slowly returned to normal, I looked at the bow tightly clutched in my left hand. I hadn't moved it! The arrow still lay peacefully across its rest. It gave no inkling that it could be a deadly weapon. In all the endless hours of practice I had never envisioned this. I had practiced to the point of perfection, or so I thought.

On that remote hillside, my brother and I found ourselves victims of "buck fever." All the time we had spent practicing hadn't prepared us as much as we thought it had done. We had just watched, almost helplessly, as a magnificent elk had walked right by us. How could this happen to us? We had spent countless hours together in the forest—hunting, hiking, and tagging along with Dad.

No matter how hard we tried to explain it, we could not. The silence of the forest was pierced by our laughter. We continued to laugh as we made our way out of the forest because we realized that practice doesn't always make perfect.

READING TO REVISE: FINDING LOGICAL ORDER

> *Remember, it is no sign of weakness or defeat that your manuscript ends up in need of major surgery. This is a common occurrence in all writing, and among the best writers.*
>
> —E. B. WHITE

Scene: You (the writer) and you (the reader) alone with your rough draft. Several moments of silence pass.

"Hmmmmmmmmm."

"That's it? That's all you've got to say?"

You scan the paper once again. "Okay, I follow this. What more do you want from me?"

"Well, for starters, some *response.* I mean, how am I doing? Does it make any sense? Should I scrap it?"

"I'm just one reader, of course—"

"Sure, I understand that."

"And I'm a friend of yours. You can't expect a fully objective reading from someone like me."

You sigh with exasperation. "You're all I've got."

"But I don't want to say anything that might—uh—jeopardize our friendship."

"I understand that—really. But I'm *asking* for advice."

"Okay," the reader says. "Fair enough."

You (the reader) scan your paper a third and final time as you (the writer) wait not-so-patiently, just on the edge of irritation, wondering why the reading has to take so long. I mean, why not just get on with it? After all, you haven't got all day.

Suddenly the reader glances up from the text. "Hey, would you *relax?* Reading with care takes *time.* Just like writing."

You swallow the dryness in your mouth. "So what do you think?"

"I think you've got a great start."

"Really?"

"Yeah, really. I mean, you're not finished yet—there's room for revision and editing—but I *like* this."

You lean forward, ready to jot down some notes.

"Work on rearranging these ideas," the reader says, "and cut away ones you don't need. Concentrate on logical order—moving from general to specific points."

"Say what?"

"General to specific. Trust me, I'm a reader—"

"But how will I know whether these changes work? I mean, suppose they don't—"

"I'm right *here*," the reader within says. "Turn to me anytime. I'll tell you whether your text makes general-to-specific sense. In fact, I'll read it as many times as you want—as long as you treat me right."

You feel encouraged. "I can't tell you how much I appreciate—"

"Hey," the reader smiles. "Don't mention it. I mean, what are friends for? Work on logical order and you'll do fine."

CHAPTER PREVIEW

In Chapter 1 you used questions to add details and support while revising. This chapter focuses on the problem of finding **logical order** in paragraphs. You'll learn to reorganize sentences so that meaning emerges, level by level; then you'll see how to cut unneeded material.

The writer George Orwell once said that "good writing is like a windowpane." What Orwell *didn't* say was that just as you need a frame for a windowpane, you also need a logical framework for revision. The basic assumption here is that by developing skill in "framing" single paragraphs, you learn to revise sequences of paragraphs.

This chapter explores levels of generality through discussion and examples—first words and phrases, then whole sentences. From the framework created by this concept, you'll come to understand the ideas of coordination and subordination and see how these principles can guide your revising work, helping you to think about logical order.

Work through the exercises in this chapter carefully, checking your answers. Our aim here, as elsewhere, is to develop reading skills that you can apply to your writing in progress. More specifically, the aim here is to offer you a kind of x-ray vision that you can use as a do-it-yourself revision tool.

LEVELS OF GENERALITY

Look at any page of printed text—this one, say—and you will see paragraphs stacked one atop another, neat and tidy. What you don't see is the structure *within* the paragraphs, the invisible "levels" of ideas.

Yet these levels exist just as surely as the subatomic particles that make up our physical world. They enable us to think and communicate. Understanding more about these levels will help you greatly as you do prose surgery. Such levels of structure are like a medical surgeon's knowledge of anatomy—absolutely essential for day-to-day work.

The idea of **levels of generality** is already familiar to you. You use it whenever you address an envelope—moving from a person's name to street address, to city and state, and (if necessary) country. What the post office does is read your envelope in reverse order, starting with the *highest* level of generality (the bottom of the envelope) and working back, step by step, to get mail to its destination.

At some point in the future, as world population expands and other planets are colonized, we may include more information on our envelopes. But the post office will still work through the levels of generality to deliver (or lose) our mail.

1. Designated solar system

   2. Specific planet or interstellar coordinates

      3. International alliance or space territory

         4. State, province, or space locale

            5. City or space station

               6. Tribal unit or social group

                  7. Mailbox coordinates

                     8. Person's number

                       9. Name

So levels of generality is a technique for sorting mail. Each level narrows the geographic range and specifies a "target" from an array of possibilities. But the same principle also underlies human language—and memory—as higher levels "package" information from lower levels. You can think of your own thinking as a hierarchy, ranging from sensory events at the "bottom" to abstractions at the "top."

To illustrate this principle in language, let's consider the following two examples:

1. Food sources	1. Food sources
2. Plants	2. Animals
3. Fruit	3. Cattle
4. Citrus	4. Herefords
5. Oranges	5. Alice

Working up from the bottom, the examples show that each word is a subset of a larger category, which in turn is a subset of another. Thus, each level has been "packaged" so that it nests within others.

SEEING LEVELS OF GENERALITY

For practice in seeing levels of generality on your own, work through the following exercises. For each pair of words, choose the "top" (superordinate) level and write that word in the "1" line; write the "lower" (subordinate) level word in the "2" line. *Note:* What may be **general** (the top level) in one context may be **specific** in another context.

EXERCISE 2.1: TWO LEVELS OF GENERALITY

Vegetables
Broccoli

1. _____

2. _____

Cobras
Snakes

1. _____

2. _____

Writing
Communication

1. _____

2. _____

Joy
Emotion

1. _____

2. _____

Investments
Real estate

1. _____

2. _____

Marshland
Real estate

1. _____

2. _____

Jazz	Jazz
Music	New wave

1. _____ 1. _____

   2. _____   2. _____

Boating	Boating
Sailing	Recreation

1. _____ 1. _____

   2. _____   2. _____

Now check your answers against the ones that follow. Notice that level of generality depends on a *relationship* between at least two ideas. As the terms of the relationship change, so does an item's level of generality.

Level 1	**Level 2**
Vegetables	Broccoli
Snakes	Cobras
Communication	Writing
Emotion	Joy
Investments	Real estate
Real estate	Marshland
Music	Jazz
Jazz	New wave
Boating	Sailing
Recreation	Boating

The levels we've considered so far show **subordination.** That is, each lower level is a subset of a higher level. But sometimes items are at the same level, not different ones. An important and related concept, then, is **coordination,** which refers to two or more items at the same level of generality. To practice spotting coordination, work through the exercises that follow. For each group of three words, two are at the "2" level.

EXERCISE 2.2: TWO LEVELS OF GENERALITY

Sofa

Furniture

Table

1. _____

   2. _____

   2. _____

Honda

Harley-Davidson

Motorcycles

1. _____

   2. _____

   2. _____

House

Apartment

Residence

1. _____

   2. _____

   2. _____

Intelligence

Verbal

Mechanical

1. _____

   2. _____

   2. _____

Pastry

Dessert

Ice cream

1. _____

   2. _____

   2. _____

Cooperation

Competition

Values

1. _____

   2. _____

   2. _____

Oriental	Revise
Caucasian	Writing process
Race	Draft

1. _____   1. _____

   2. _____   2. _____

   2. _____   2. _____

Litter	Coordinate
Bottles	Levels of ideas
Paper	Subordinate

1. _____   1. _____

   2. _____   2. _____

   2. _____   2. _____

As you can see from the above practice, coordination refers to items at the same level of generality; subordination refers to items at different levels. Now check your answers against these.

Level 1	Level 2	Level 2
Furniture	Table	Sofa
Motorcycles	Harley-Davidson	Honda
Residence	Apartment	House
Intelligence	Verbal	Mechanical
Dessert	Pastry	Ice cream
Values	Cooperation	Competition
Race	Oriental	Caucasian
Writing process	Draft	Revise
Litter	Bottles	Paper
Levels of ideas	Coordinate	Subordinate

Let's take one more step to develop background on levels of generality. In the exercise that follows, test your understanding of coordination and subordination. Fill in words that seem to fit at the appropriate levels. After doing the exercise, check the possible answers that follow; yours may differ. Also, check with other students to see how they completed the exercise. Be prepared to discuss the reasons for your various answers in class.

EXERCISE 2.3: MORE LEVELS OF GENERALITY

1. Snacks
  2. Pretzels
  2. _____
    3. _____

1. _____
  2. Bikes
  2. Cars
    3. _____

---

1. _____
  2. Soft drinks
    3. Root beer
    3. _____

1. Technology
  2. Computers
    3. _____
    3. _____

---

1. Summer jobs
  2. Outdoor
  2. _____
    3. _____

1. Books
  2. Biography
  2. _____
    3. _____

---

1. _____
  2. Essay
  2. _____
    3. True-false
    3. _____

1. Family
  2. _____
  2. Parents
    3. _____
    3. _____

1. Contemporary music
   2. _____
      3. Willie Nelson
      3. Alabama
   2. Classical music
      3. _____
      3. _____
   2. _____
      3. _____
      3. _____

1. Modern politics
   2. _____
      3. U.S.A.
      3. _____
      3. _____
   2. _____
      3. U.S.S.R.
      3. _____
      3. _____
   2. Developing nations

Level 1	Level 2	Level 3
Snacks	Pretzels/Fruit	Apples
Transportation	Bikes/Cars	Ford
Beverages	Soft drinks	Root beer/Cola
Technology	Computers	IBM/Apple
Summer jobs	Outdoor/Indoor	Typist
Books	Biography/Fiction	*Huckleberry Finn*
Exams	Essay/Objective	True-False/ Matching
Family	Siblings/Parents	Mother/Father
Contemporary music	Country music	Willie Nelson/ Alabama
	Classical music	Bach/Mozart
	Pop music	Madonna/ Prince
Modern politics	Democratic nations	U.S.A./Japan/ England
	Communist nations	U.S.S.R./China/ Cuba

COORDINATE-SEQUENCE PARAGRAPHS

All of this practice with coordination and subordination has been building background for work with paragraphs. In other words, the level-of-generality principles you've learned also apply to sentences.

Our aim is to see paragraph structure more clearly by grouping sentences into logical levels. We'll first consider a paragraph with a coordinate sequence as its method of development. (Please note that this paragraph serves as an introduction for each of the illustrative paragraphs that follow later in this chapter.)

 INTRODUCTION TO "MODEL SCHOOLS" (COORDINATE SEQUENCE)

1. According to research, schools that promote learning share several characteristics.

2. They employ teachers who have high expectations of students.

2. These schools are led by principals who value academic learning and work to achieve it.

2. They emphasize the "basics," though not necessarily "drill and practice."

2. Such schools maintain an orderly environment that promotes healthy classroom interchange.

2. Their testing programs provide feedback to teachers and students about progress toward goals.

As you can see, this **coordinate-sequence paragraph** has a general organizing sentence—a **topic sentence**—at level 1. This paragraph also has a series of sentences that name five characteristics of schools that promote learning. These five sentences are **parallel.** That is, they are all at the same level of generality. This kind of organization is often called **parallel structure.**

Coordinate sequence is a very powerful way of expressing ideas. First comes a main idea; then come a number of supporting points. The speeches of Martin Luther King, Jr., or the Reverend Jesse Jackson—speeches that galvanized millions of Americans to support civil rights causes—are excellent examples of coordinate sequence (or parallel structure) in action.

Notice in our example that the five sentences begin with slightly different words or phrases—"they," "these schools," "such schools," "their testing programs." Yet, in spite of these differences in form, the ideas behind the words seem to be at the same level, all pointing to the word "schools" at level 1. From this example you can see that sentences don't have to be identical in structure to be parallel. But they do have to be at the same level of generality.

To check your understanding of coordinate sequence, let's take the sentence about teachers from the paragraph and develop it into a paragraph of its own. Read the following sentences carefully, thinking about levels of generality. Look first for the most general (level-1) sentence. Then reorganize the list. Put the identifying letters for the sentences in a coordinate sequence, with the most general sentence—the topic sentence—at the top and the others arranged in a way that seems most effective to you.

EXERCISE 2.4: THE TEACHERS
(Coordinate Sequence—Reorganizing Practice)

A. They may reward students for thinking and not just "following along."

B. Their feedback to students may emphasize a need for "more effort" when work is not up to standard.

C. Teachers communicate their expectations of students in subtle ways.

D. Teachers may pay attention to the students who work hard rather than concentrating only on troublemakers.

E. In spite of pressure, they hold fast to homework deadlines rather than giving in.

  1. _____

   2. ____

   2. ____

   2. ____

   2. ____

Sentence C is the most general one; and one effective sequence for the exercise is this one: 1.C, 2.A, 2.B, 2.E, 2.D. However, you may have arranged your coordinate sequence in a slightly different way.

SUBORDINATE-SEQUENCE PARAGRAPHS

Having introduced coordinate-sequence paragraphing, let's switch to subordinate sequence. We'll first look at a model paragraph, then practice arranging sentences into levels.

THE PRINCIPAL
(Subordinate Sequence)

1. A principal sets the academic tone for a school.

 2. As an instructional leader, this individual values achievement and encourages teachers to do the same.

  3. For example, the principal may honor teachers for teaching excellence.

   4. Such recognition helps everyone to understand the aims of the school.

  3. Also, the principal may deemphasize athletics and social activities.

4. This is accomplished through budgeting priorities and scheduling decisions.

Notice that the paragraph begins with a general topic sentence at level 1. Level 2 is more specific. The first sentence at level 3 is even more specific, providing an example. The first sentence at level 4 "shifts down" further, telling the *effect* (or result) of the level-3 action. Then the paragraph shifts *up* to a second example at level 3, one parallel to the earlier one. The follow-up sentence at level 4 tells what causes the effect in the previous level.

If you pay attention to the wording, you'll see some signals for the downshifting of levels. For example, notice "this individual" (referring to the principal), "for example" (announcing an illustration), "such recognition" (pointing to honoring teachers), "this" (referring to deemphasizing athletics and social activities). Each downshift becomes slightly more specific. The "upshift" for the second level-3 sentence becomes slightly more general. Its signal is "also" (announcing a second example).

To check your understanding of subordinate sequence in paragraphs, read the following sentences carefully. Think about their levels of generality. Then put the identifying letters for the sentences in the blanks in a sequence that makes the most sense to you. Take your time with this exercise.

EXERCISE 2.5: THE BASICS
(Subordinate Sequence—Reorganizing Practice)

A. The term *basics* refers to skills such as reading and writing.

B. Effective schools emphasize the basics.

C. In SSR, everyone in the school reads for a few minutes at the same time every day.

D. A school may reinforce reading by establishing a Sustained Silent Reading (SSR) program.

E. In WAC, writing becomes a tool for learning in all classes, not just English.

F. A school may reinforce writing by encouraging writing across the curriculum (WAC).

1. ____

  2. ____

    3. ____

      4. ____

    3. ____

      4. ____

You may have found this exercise difficult. Now compare your sequence with this one: 1.B, 2.A, 3.D, 4.C, 3.F, 4.E. Let's consider, point by point, why the sentences are listed in this order.

Sentence B is at level 1 because it is the most general sentence of the group (the topic sentence). Sentence A is at level 2 because it defines a key term in the level-1 sentence, the term *basics*. D is the *first* level-3 sentence because reading is the first idea in level 2. F is the *second* level-3 sentence because *writing* is the second idea in level 2. C is the first level-4 sentence because it defines a key term (*Sustained Silent Reading*) in the first level-3 sentence. E is the second level-4 sentence because it explains a key term (*writing across the curriculum*) in the second level-3 sentence.

Notice the two sentences at level 3. Although these sentences are parallel (or coordinate), their parallelism occurs in a larger subordinate-sequence format. This point is discussed more fully in the next section of this chapter.

Notice, too, that it would not be a good idea to reverse the order of the two sentences at level 3. Because the order of ideas in level 2 is reading and writing, follow-up sentences should follow this order so that the paragraph will be easy to read. Reversing the order in the follow-up sentences would probably cause difficulty for a reader.

MORE PRACTICE WITH SENTENCE LEVELS

As you've seen, *coordinate sequence* and *subordinate sequence* are relative terms. A coordinate-sequence paragraph usually has at least one level of subordination. Why? Because any shift down from level 1 is, by definition, subordination. By the same token, a subordinate-sequence paragraph often has one or more sentences that are parallel to each other.

In other words, many paragraphs have a mixed sequence—with elements of *both* coordination and subordination. The concluding practice focuses your attention on both strategies. This exercise is slightly more difficult than the earlier ones. Study it carefully, thinking about how sentence levels fit together to make a coherent whole.

EXERCISE 2.6: THE ENVIRONMENT
(Mixed Sequence—Reorganizing Practice)

A. "Order" does not mean that the school is authoritarian or repressive.

B. It simply means that students respect teachers and that teachers respect students.

C. Good schools maintain an orderly environment.

D. Students who disrupt the classroom learn that such behavior is not permitted.

E. Teachers who abuse their power are reminded of school policies.

F. Consequences for misbehavior follow from a clear set of classroom rules.

G. The principal or supervisor helps the teacher to find better ways of working.

  1. ____

    2. ____

    2. ____

      3. ____

        4. ____

      3. ____

        4. ____

Now compare your answers with these: 1.C, 2.A, 2.B, 3.D, 4.F, 3.E, 4.G. Sentences A and B are both at level 2 because they both define a key term—"orderly environment"—in sentence C, the topic sentence. At level 3, sentence D focuses on one idea ("students respect teachers") in the previous sentence, B. The following sentence, F, further explains the consequence of D. At the next level 3, sentence E focuses on the second idea in the earlier level-2 sentence ("teachers respecting students"). Its follow-up sentence, G, further explains the consequence of E.

This paragraph is a **mixed sequence** because it uses both **coordination** and **subordination** as organizing strategies. Here is a final practice paragraph, again a mixed sequence. Pay special attention to your sequencing of items at level 3.

EXERCISE 2.7: EVALUATION
(Mixed Sequence—Reorganizing Practice)

A. "Good evaluation" means the assessment of progress, not just grading.

B. In summary, evaluation operates at all levels of an effective school.

C. The principal needs to assess the strengths and weaknesses of the program.

D. An alert community needs to ensure that the school board makes wise decisions.

E. The final characteristic of an effective school is good evaluation.

F. Students need to know where they stand academically.

G. Teachers need to see the progress of individuals toward learning goals.

   1. ____

      2. ____

         3. ____

         3. ____

         3. ____

         3. ____

   1. ____

Now compare your answers with these: 1.E, 2.A, 3.F, 3.G, 3.C, 3.D, 1.B. Notice that this paragraph has both an introductory topic sentence and a general clincher sentence at its conclusion. Note, too, the logical sequencing of points at level 3—students, teachers, principal, community. What order did you choose for these ideas? While this paragraph has some subordination, it is primarily a coordinate-sequence paragraph.

CUTTING UNNEEDED MATERIAL

So far you've seen how to reorganize sentences, level by level, so that logical order emerges clearly. But there's a second approach based on the levels-of-generality principle. This approach involves *cutting* ideas and examples that don't really fit.

For an example, let's return to the sequence of sentences that opened our work with sentence levels in this chapter.

INTRODUCTION TO "MODEL SCHOOLS"
(Coordinate Sequence)

1. According to research, schools that promote learning share several characteristics.

2. They employ teachers who have high expectations of students.

2. These schools are led by principals who value academic learning and work to achieve it.

2. They emphasize the "basics," though not necessarily "drill and practice."

2. Such schools maintain an orderly environment that promotes healthy classroom interchange.

2. Their testing programs provide feedback to teachers and students about progress toward goals.

This paragraph provided an introduction to the five paragraphs of explanation we worked with in this chapter. In other words, each of the five follow-up paragraphs explained in greater detail one of the coordinate sentences in the introduction. The follow-up paragraphs make up the body of the paper.

Let's suppose, however, that in our draft for this paper we've written some additional material.

1. The public schools in Japan, where illiteracy is almost unknown, are quite different from those in the United States.

2. The Japanese Ministry of Education has a uniform national curriculum, which all schools must follow.

2. All students, regardless of ability, are expected to acquire the same information on the same schedule.

2. Parents enroll their children in enrichment programs, supervise their homework, and communicate with their teachers.

2. Japanese students go to school about three weeks per year more than American students.

2. Teachers are accorded high respect and high salaries in Japan.

The preceding coordinate-sequence paragraph concerns schools, of course, but is it directly relevant to the focus of the introduction? As matters stand, you'd either have to revise the introductory paragraph or delete the material on Japanese schools. While these points are interesting and potentially useful, they simply don't fit here.

Having good paragraphs that don't fit is a basic problem as you revise. When you've worked hard to generate and draft an idea, you feel a strong urge to include it, one way or another. Resist this temptation. Nothing undermines revision more surely than including irrelevant ideas. Unless you're prepared to revise your basic aims so that the material will fit, you're better off taking a clearheaded, hard-nosed approach.

For practice in spotting unnecessary material—a sentence that doesn't belong—let's look at a conclusion for our "Model Schools" essay. Like any **concluding paragraph,** this one is supposed to restate or expand key points of the introduction. Find a sentence in Exercise 2.8 that should be cut because it doesn't fit.

EXERCISE 2.8: CONCLUSION TO "MODEL SCHOOLS"
(Cutting Unneeded Material)

1. The task of improving our public schools is enormous, but the general plan for doing so seems fairly clear.

2. Teachers need to have high expectations of their students and to be led by administrators who value academic learning, not merely success on the athletic field.

2. Programs need to emphasize "basics," such as Sustained Silent Reading (SSR) and writing across the curriculum (WAC), with appropriate and meaningful feedback to students and teachers.

2. Classrooms need to be orderly places where students respect teachers and teachers respect students so that real learning can occur.

2. Sensible and humane programs of evaluation must operate at all levels, not just in classrooms.

2. Parents must play an active role in motivating and encouraging children and in supporting the efforts of teachers.

1. By implementing these ideas, public schools will help to create a solid and secure future for our democratic way of life.

If you chose the next-to-the-last sentence, concerning parents, as the one to cut, you're correct. That's a new idea being introduced at the conclusion of the essay. Because it hasn't been developed in the earlier paragraphs of the paper, it should be deleted.

"But wait a minute," you protest. "Parental involvement *has* to be there if we hope to improve American schools!"

You're right, of course. So keep this sentence about parents. But make sure to revise the introduction and the body of the paper to reflect this new idea. Writing a new paragraph on parental involvement and inserting it into the text would be an excellent revision strategy. As matters now stand, this new paragraph would be placed following Exercise 2.7, Evaluation.

LOOKING BACK, LOOKING AHEAD

The principle of levels of generality is a powerful revising tool for writing that explains or persuades. As we've seen, when you have several points at the same level or simply want to repeat a single point for emphasis, you'll probably use a coordinate sequence (also called *parallelism*). On the other hand, when you want to develop an idea through subtopics, examples, and follow-up details, you'll probably use a *subordinate sequence*.

Work through the following exercises, comparing your reorganized sentences with those given by your instructor. Your answers may not always agree, but you'll still develop a *feel* for logical paragraphs. Then move to Exercise 2.13 and analyze a section of your writing in progress (or a finished paper) in terms of levels. This work will help you apply these ideas for revising.

The levels-of-generality principle is a kind of x-ray for looking at prose structure. Used intelligently, it can help you identify topic sentences, create a "frame" for revision, and make decisions about whether material should be cut. In Chapter 3, you'll learn more about the hidden structure of text by examining six basic types of paragraphs.

 **DO-IT-YOURSELF EXERCISES**

Please be prepared to share your work in class. Your instructor will provide suggested answers for Exercises 2.9–2.12. Use Exercise 2.13 to make a personal application of the levels-of-generality principle.

EXERCISE 2.9: THREE LEVELS OF GENERALITY

Directions: Arrange the three words in each set below; then add an appropriate level-3 item that fits the context.

Automobiles	Squirrels
Compacts	Rodents
Toyotas	Animals

1. _____   1. _____
   2. _____   2. _____
     3. _____   3. _____
     3. _____   3. _____

Fast foods   TV set
Nutrition   Entertainment
Pizza   Recreation

1. _____   1. _____
   2. _____   2. _____
     3. _____   3. _____
     3. _____   3. _____

Religions   Mental health
Methodists   Depression
Christianity   Crying

1. _____   1. _____
   2. _____   2. _____
     3. _____   3. _____
     3. _____   3. _____

Reading skills   Skimming techniques
General education   Improving speed
Language education   Reading skills

1. _____   1. _____
   2. _____   2. _____
     3. _____   3. _____
     3. _____   3. _____

EXERCISE 2.10: SCHOOL DISRUPTION
(Reorganizing Practice)

Directions: Reorganize the following sentences by putting appropriate letters in the numbered blanks below them. When you finish doing this activity, be prepared to say whether the paragraph would fit logically into the sequence of paragraphs you developed in this chapter. If so, where?

A. The second source of disruption comes from the school itself.

B. These students divert the attention of everyone from matters at hand.

C. Disruption in classrooms comes from two major sources.

D. Bells and buzzers, intercom announcements, office messengers, pep assemblies, hall passes and other paperwork—all distract from the learning process.

E. The first is from students who are bored, hostile, or more interested in each other than in learning.

F. They talk out, fool around, make fun of others, cause fights, or socialize.

G. In fact, some schools seem better organized to *promote* disruption than to prevent it.

    1. ____

      2. ____

        3. ____

        3. ____

      2. ____

        3. ____

        3. ____

EXERCISE 2.11: SCHOOL HISTORY
(Reorganizing Practice)

Directions: Reorganize the following sentences by putting appropriate letters in the numbered blanks below them. When you finish doing this activity, be prepared to say whether this paragraph would fit logically into the sequence of paragraphs you developed in this chapter. If so, where?

A. Michigan, in 1870, became the first state to make public education free.

B. Prior to 1870, all United States "public" schools charged tuition.

C. Many families could not afford the fees of these public schools.

D. Free public education and compulsory attendance are relatively recent developments in our nation's history.

E. In fact, attending public school was once a privilege, not a right.

F. Mandatory school attendance finally became a national policy in 1918.

G. In 1872, the U.S. Supreme Court ruled that public funds should be spent on high schools.

H. Therefore, about half the children in the United States were not attending school in 1870.

I. By 1900, over half the states had laws requiring youths to attend school until the age of 14.

1. ____

2. ____

3. ____

4. ____

4. ____

3. ____

3. ____

3. ____

3. ____

EXERCISE 2.12: DETACHMENT
(Cutting Unneeded Material)

Directions: Read through the following eight-sentence paragraph and circle *two* sentences that probably don't fit the logical order. Be prepared to say why these sentences should be cut from the paragraph.

1. At 32,000 feet, passengers heard the roar of jet engines as a muffled, silken purr.

2. They sedated themselves with cocktails and leaned back to thumb through magazines.

2. Yawning, they rode a cushion of air at 500 miles per hour, bored by the miracle of flight.

3. Now that I think about it, I was pretty sleepy myself.

1. Outside, meanwhile, the temperature was 50 degrees below zero.

2. White moonlight silvered the snowy landscape far below.

2. Far off in the distance, tiny points of lights mirrored a night sky filled with glittering stars.

3. "Twinkle, twinkle, little star/How I wonder what you are."

EXERCISE 2.13: PERSONAL APPLICATION

This chapter has introduced you to levels of generality. During revision, this principle can help you add new ideas, reorganize existing sentences, or cut unneeded material.

To apply what you've learned about levels of generality, reread a completed paper or a draft of writing in progress. Find two consecutive paragraphs that read well and photocopy them. Then find two paragraphs that need revision and make photocopies of them.

Outline the effective paragraphs as demonstrated in this chapter. First, identify sentences in each paragraph by letter (A, B, C, D, etc.). Then, underline the topic sentence in each paragraph. Finally, on a separate sheet of paper, begin the process of indenting, level by level. You don't have to rewrite the sentences; just put their identifying letters (A, B, C, D, etc.) in the appropriate spaces.

Your first task for the problem paragraphs is to underline the topic sentence (if available) in each paragraph. Then, on a separate sheet of paper, go to work revising the paragraphs. You can add new sentences that seem to fit logically, rearrange existing sentences, or cut unneeded ones. Keep the principle of levels of generality in mind as you work.

Now look back at the "before" and "after" versions of your problem paragraphs. What was the basis for the changes you made? Were there "breaks" in the levels of generality? Did you create additional levels? Did you switch your arrangement from coordination to subordination—or vice versa? Did you lack sentences at the lower, more specific levels? Did you cut unneeded sentences? Write about the revisions you made and why you made them.

Hand in your work from this application activity. Your packet of materials should contain the following: (1) photocopies of four original paragraphs—two effective ones, two in need of revision; (2) your outline of levels for the effective paragraphs; (3) your revisions of the two problem paragraphs; and (4) your follow-up writing about the changes you made and the reasons for those changes.

 **PROSE SURGERY IN ACTION**

In this illustration of prose surgery, watch Cynthia Harmer
cut and reorganize as she develops a personal essay. Included
are two early versions of her opening paragraphs. Following
these working drafts is the paper Cynthia eventually read
aloud in class. Her changes resulted from work with a peer-
response group as well as from conferences.

In the first draft, Cynthia writes four paragraphs just to
get us to Grandpa's house. In her revision, she tightens the
focus, sets the scene more clearly, and introduces us to
Grandpa. In her final paper, she reorganizes again—sharpen-
ing the focus further by putting us immediately *in* the situation, spinning out her narrative, and drawing her conclusions. Notice the strength of her voice in the final version.

An interesting feature of Cynthia's final essay is her han-
dling of time. Within one memory—visiting Grandpa at harvest time—is embedded an earlier memory of planting potatoes. Note also the many stylistic changes (and the variety
of sentence-level corrections) that Cynthia makes as she
brings her essay along. She found that reading her work
aloud helped her make a variety of revising and editing decisions.

Here are the four symbols used in class and in conferences
to prompt revision and editing:

   + = I like this [word, phrase, sentence].

   √ = Please check this [word, phrase, sentence].

   ? = I don't follow this [word, phrase, sentence].

   # = Think about developing this part more.

Grandpa's House
(Response Group Draft)

I can still hear Dad's irritated voice echoeing distinctively through evry room in the house. "Come on let's go. We are going to be late." My brothers and I were rushed into the plush, blue, continental car in an attempt to save precious time.

Today was the day! A day I had personally looked forward to for weeks. We were off to visit Grandpa Harmer in Mapleton. I anxiously looked forward to the anticipated time of arrival which was now five minutes behind schedule.

The slow, smooth, moving ride seemed to last forever. I was growing increasingly more impatient. "How long until we get there." I asked. "Soon, now please sit down." Father replied. I had two motive for asking this question. First, I wanted to see Grandpa. Second I was presently being scrunched between my two bickering brothers.

I noticed in the distance coming closer as the minutes past was the old familiar roads. The smell of manure filled my nostrils and I quickly relaxed. So much did the old faded signs and cow filled pastures fill me with the tangible security that was so needed in my life then.

[This goes on to describe the arrival at the house and subsequent work in the fields.]

Grandpa's Fields
(Conference Draft)

fragment Today was the day! [A day I had anticipated for weeks!] "We're here. Everybody out!" Mom and Dad and my two younger brothers shouted in unison. My family and I immediately pieled out of the blue, continental car and headed toward Grandpa's quarter acre corn fields that lie adjacent to his small one-story brick house.

At eight, the world was a fascinating place. I wanted to see and experience as much of it as humanly possible. First, I noticed the familiar browness of Mapleton's small country town. Soft mahogany shades covered the rough, rigid mountains far in the distance. A thin layer of dust blanketed the paved road nearby. As I strolled behind my brothers, Greg and Matt, stepping in my father's huge black shadow, I watched the next *fragment* door neighbor's young colt. [Whose rich auburn mane toosled *cliché* in the cool evening breeze.]

Grandpa Harmer called out to greet us. "Hello!" he said with *fragment* a thick drawl in his voice. [A drawl identical to my own father's.] Grandpa was a short, stonchy, old man. [Who wore fadded, worn, *fragment* levi overalls with a burgandy handercheif in the left back pocket.] As he walked, I saw a slight limp from a stroke he had a few years ago. Grandpa's irriplaceable crooked smile was deepened by several wrinkles.

comma splice I was Grandpa's favorite granddaughter. I knew it, infact ; in fact, the whole family knew it. His smile brightened as he saw my face pertruding out from under my Father's arm. Grandpa's *?* large, sturdy frame accompanied and almost contradicted his mild-mannered style. All I knew is was that he provided the extra special attention I thrived on. I loved to visit Grandpa even though my brothers and I had to come.

[This draft goes on to describe working in the fields and Cynthia's relationship with her grandfather.]

Grandpa's Fields
by
Cynthia Harmer

Soft mahogany shades covered the rough mountains far in the distance. A thin layer of dust blanketed the paved road nearby. As I strolled behind my brothers, Greg and Matt, stepping in my father's huge shadow, I watched the next door neighbor's young colt. His rich auburn mane caught my attention.

Grandpa Harmer called out to greet us with a thick drawl identical to my father's. Grandpa was a short, stocky old man. He wore faded Levi overalls with a burgundy handkerchief in the left back pocket. He walked with a slight limp from a stroke he had suffered a few years earlier. Grandpa's crooked smile, deepened by wrinkles, was creased by the touch of time.

I was Grandpa's favorite eight-year-old granddaughter. I knew it; in fact, the whole family knew it. His smile brightened as he saw my face. Grandpa's large sturdy frame contradicted his mild-mannered style. All I knew was that he provided the extra special attention I thrived on. Even though my brothers and I were obliged to come, I loved to visit Grandpa.

The September harvest season was now upon us, but I remembered the work we had done on our last visit in March, giving Grandpa a hand in his backyard field. It was more like an extended garden than a farm. On that day I had planted potatoes with Grandpa.

As Grandpa's personal assistant, I followed him down several rows, waiting as he hoed a place for the small potato pieces I held in my even smaller hands. I felt the gritty starch as I reached into the white plastic bucket, adding small amounts of dirt each time I did. My fair skin had reddened in the noonday sunshine. I wiped the sweat from my face, getting dirt all over it and in my stringy blonde hair. I loved it! This was a great excuse to get dirty without getting in trouble.

Now, as I finished reminiscing about last March, I looked around me. Today we had come to help Grandpa Harmer pick his crops and take some home with us. It felt good to be with Grandpa again. We all headed toward the corn field. The tall green stalks enclosed me as I brushed by the limp, leafy branches. Grandpa loaded me up with ten corn cobs to take to his kitchen.

A rust-colored sunset spread across the sky as we finished loading corn into Grandpa's kitchen and the backseat of our car. I then went to see what progress had transpired in Grandpa's backyard quarter-acre field since I had last visited. Soon, I knew, we would be picking crops out of this garden.

The old apple tree was full of ripe, juicy apples. The gray chain-link fence was almost indistinguishable from the twisting grape vines and red raspberry plants. Watermelons and pumpkins grew nearby. The red potatoes Grandpa and I had spent so much time planting were flourishing throughout the garden. Tonight I would take a big box of what I thought were the finest tasting potatoes I too had helped grow.

Grandpa Harmer stood beside me, placing his massive arm around my tiny shoulders. Together we looked over the garden with a renewed pride. He kidded me, but beneath our conversation were voices not heard with ears. The quiet whispers of "I love you" flowed from his heart to mine and back again like a secret carried by the wind. Although my ears would never hear those words, I knew in the silence they were there.

A year later Grandpa came to live with us, and for whatever reason, we never went back to his fields. He wasn't happy without his land. He was a man who had built his life with hard work and great care. Farming was a long-kept family tradition he held on to for his life's satisfaction.

The desperation I felt for my now unhappy grandfather saddened me. I didn't understand the pain that manifested itself through his harsh words and frowns. I remembered our times in his garden and wished I could give back to him what he had lost. I loved him. Grandpa stayed with us until he died, a few months later.

Now, each time I pass by freshly cut green grass I think of Grandpa. His crooked smile stands out in my mind. I learned from him what it meant to be accepted and loved and never to be afraid of hard work. Grandpa and I did more in those days than pick corn and plant potatoes—we planted memories.

READING TO REVISE: TINKERING WITH PARAGRAPHS

> *Now get out your sharpest pencil or your favorite pen and be ruthless. You're a surgeon—cut, add, reorder.*
>
> —DONALD MURRAY

Scene: A meeting with other students from your writing class.

You finish reading a draft. "So what do you think?" you ask. "Maybe I should start over?"

Someone shrugs. "Hey, it's not that bad."

"Yeah, pretty good," another person adds. "Really."

A shuffling silence follows. You wonder how to get your response group to say more. "The opening part—" you nudge. "I mean, can you follow what I'm getting at?"

"Uhm, I'm not sure," a brave soul ventures.

You wait, hoping for some specific advice.

Finally the brave soul looks up. "I say you're clearing your throat with the opening paragraph. You sure you really need it?"

"I spent an hour on it."

"So? Why not use your example up front—I mean, to introduce what you're going to say? Like, uh, get the reader's attention. Cut what you don't need and move the sentences around. Just tinker a little—"

You scribble a note to yourself: "Tinker with paragraphs."

Some members of the group are rereading your paper.

"I had to reread the middle part to get the meaning," a friend volunteers. "Everything's there, but maybe numbering the points would help—I don't know."

"More tinkering then."

"Yeah, so the transitions are clear."

"And break it up into paragraphs," another person suggests. "It's hard to read a page that isn't in chunks."

"Chunks?"

"Yeah, you know—paragraph chunks."

"The end paragraph is great," someone adds. "I could *see* it happening, step by step—"

"Uh-huh."

"I said to myself, 'Okay, here comes this comparison'."

"But I never followed through."

"Right—I'm still waiting."

"Okay, I need to add that—"

"A little cutting and rearranging," the brave soul says. "The ideas are fine. I mean, interesting, you know? Like I said, maybe just some tinkering on paragraphs."

"Tinkering," you murmur aloud, wondering how to proceed.

"Yeah," they nod. "You got it."

CHAPTER PREVIEW

This chapter focuses on the problem of adding, cutting, and reorganizing sentences to create patterns that readers can follow. The task you'll face—first thinking about an emerging meaning, then tinkering with sentences in the context of paragraphs—is basic to the larger process of revising or editing your prose.

As with question asking in Chapter 1 and levels of generality in Chapter 2, we'll zero in on paragraph-level revision, for three reasons. First, skill with paragraphs is essential for success with longer units of text—reports, essay exams, letters, and proposals. Second, paragraphs are easier to study than whole texts, yet the processes for revising them (adding, cutting, reorganizing) are the same. And third, many paragraphs have clear patterns (like the numerical-order pattern you're now reading). Being able to recognize and use such basic patterns can help you discover your meanings as you revise.

You'll see that though there are no "right" answers when it comes to revising paragraph patterns, some answers are better than others. The real aim of this chapter is to help you *think* as you revise—making meanings clear to yourself first, then to your reader. What you'll consider are basic logical relationships between ideas.

THINKING ABOUT PARAGRAPHS

Before exploring patterns, let's think of **paragraphs** as ways to package (or "punctuate") a text into chunks of meaning. Notice in the Chapter Preview that three closely related paragraphs point to the ones you're now reading.

But why three paragraphs? Why not five or two? Why not a single paragraph of introduction? The answer has to do with intuitions—one's hunches about the needs of readers and how sentences logically "cluster" in the text. Three paragraphs *felt* right in the section above. Yet in other contexts a paragraph for special emphasis might consist of a single sentence—or even one word. A paragraph that lists a number of closely related points might run to a dozen sentences or more.

Paragraph length also depends on the type of writing being done and the format for publication. For example, brief paragraphs are usually desirable for business correspondence. Similarly, the narrow columns of newspapers demand shorter paragraphs than do typewritten reports or textbooks like this one. In rereading your prose for paragraphing, you'll need to consider such matters.

Generally speaking, the paragraphs in academic writing

contain between three and ten sentences, with five to seven sentences typical. The key, as we saw in Chapter 1, is to make the paragraphs long enough to develop a central idea or topic. Short, choppy paragraphs can be difficult to read because relationships between ideas aren't clear. On the other hand, a text without paragraphs is like a long-winded speaker—one who doesn't pause or give emphasis to key points.

As we noted in Chapter 2, expository paragraphs often have some kind of generalization or topic sentence to orient the reader and provide direction for what follows. Whenever you're trying to organize a long, unwieldy text into readable paragraphs, you'll find it helpful to search for these general statements and use them as paragraph openers. If your resulting paragraphs feel choppy and undeveloped, use the questioning techniques from Chapter 1 as a means of adding details and support.

Besides providing visual "breathers" for the reader, paragraphs provide clues to the organization of the text. In other words, each paragraph not only *says* something but *does* something. Some paragraphs introduce or forecast what is to follow, others develop points and make transitions, while still others conclude or summarize. All of these moves help make the text accessible. To tinker with paragraphs often means to clarify your introduction, transitions, or conclusion.

So far we've noted that paragraphs not only package a text into readable chunks but also introduce, develop, and summarize information. But what are the basic ways of clustering sentences into meaningful units during revision? Let's explore this question in what follows.

SIX PARAGRAPH PATTERNS

Put a tub full of blocks in front of young children, and they will sort and arrange them—creating a pattern from a confused disarray. Put sentences in front of readers and they will look for patterns of meaning. Six basic patterns for paragraphs (and combinations of paragraphs) help us structure the world of text and make sense of it.

Just as short, basic sentences can be transformed into statements that express complex and subtle ideas, simple paragraph plans can be combined to create "hybrid" patterns that will serve your writing goals. As you draft ideas, such combining happens naturally, at both the sentence and paragraph levels. During revision, however, the process becomes more deliberate as you add, delete, and reorganize.

To create both mature sentences and complex paragraphs, you must draw upon deeply internalized patterns—patterns learned from years of language experience. To illustrate these patterns, we will use six pairs of related sentences.

Look for one basic paragraph pattern in this first pair.

1. Mark slouched silently in the corner.
   To his left sat Maria, a lovely girl with dark eyes.

These sentences reveal a basic pattern in descriptive writing—namely, physical location, or **spatial order.** Words and phrases that signal this pattern include all kinds of location words and directions—*right, near the windows, outside, nearby, up ahead, below, in the distance*—that help readers understand.

Study the second pattern.

2. She turned, smiled, and then asked him what was wrong.
   After glancing at his notebook, he sighed to himself.

Because these sentences show a sequence of events, we'll call this pattern **time order.** You automatically use this pattern when narrating action or describing a process. Words such as *after, before, next, then, finally,* and *later* often signal this pattern.

What pattern do you see in the next two sentences?

3. Her beauty gave him one reason to pause.
   Forgetting her name provided another.

This third pattern is called **numerical order.** You use this pattern to list a series of related points. Signal words here include numbers (for example, *one reason*) as well as words like *another, in addition, moreover, and finally.*

Let's now consider a fourth pattern.

4. His writing assignment was at home—also forgotten.
   As a consequence, he was very depressed.

These sentences have a **cause/effect order,** one of the basic patterns for writing that explains. In this particular example, the cause is given first, the effect second; but the pattern can also be reversed. Signal words such as *consequently, because, since, so, therefore,* and *as a result* accompany this pattern.

How about the fifth pattern?

5. As usual, Maria looked stunning.
   Mark, on the other hand, looked stunned.

Compare/contrast order is the pattern here. Signal words such as *but, however, whereas, on the other hand,* and *in contrast* point to differences. Other signals—*like, similarly, also, in the same way,* and *as usual*—point to similarities.

Now study the sixth pattern.

6. His embarrassment was profound.
   In fact, his two lapses of memory made him wonder about early senility.

General/specific order is revealed here. This important workhorse pattern helps you develop generalizations with one or more examples. Signal words for this pattern include phrases such as *for example, in fact, that is, more specifically,* and *in other words.*

Are these six approaches the *only* ways to organize paragraphs? Hardly. Some paragraphs (or combinations of paragraphs) use other patterns—for example, *problem/solution* and *question/answer.* You might note that *question/answer* is the pattern used in the paragraph you're now reading.

Nevertheless, these six patterns deserve your attention because they're used so frequently. If you look closely at writing that explains or persuades, you'll find these patterns used repeatedly—often in combinations—to organize sentences into meaningful chunks. Understanding how the patterns work can help you with revision. For more information on these patterns, you may want to glance ahead now to the end of this chapter—p. 110 and following.

WORKING WITH PARAGRAPH PATTERNS

As you saw in Chapter 1, question asking is a powerful tool for adding sentences as you revise. We'll now combine what you learned there with the levels-of-generality principle you learned in Chapter 2.

Let's use the sentences about Mark and Maria as an introduction to a brief essay on human memory. To make a transition from Mark's embarrassment to the body of our essay, we might have drafted something like this:

Forgetting, as illustrated above, is hardly fun.
For this reason, I intend to discuss memory in what follows.

While such a transition gets to the point quickly, it's also quite abrupt. By answering a reader's probable questions— *How does this relate to me? Why should I read this?*—we can develop this paragraph further.

Read the draft closely and you'll see an implied cause/ effect order. To paraphrase, it says that forgetting isn't fun, so memory will be this paper's focus. In Exercise 3.1, we retain the original draft but write a stronger, more fully developed transition paragraph.

EXERCISE 3.1: MEMORY
(Adding Details and Support)

1. Forgetting, as illustrated above, is hardly fun.

   2. In fact, _____

   _____

   _____

2. Examples such as _____

_____

_____

1. For these reasons, I intend to discuss memory in what follows.

Using the framework of levels from Chapter 2, it's easy to add sentences. Compare the revision that follows with the two-sentence paragraph we started with. Which holds interest, sounds authoritative, and feels like better writing?

1. Forgetting, as illustrated above, is hardly fun.

   2. In fact, memory lapses can and do lead to moments of anger and embarrassment for everyone.

   2. Forgetting car keys, appointments, or the names of people to whom we were just introduced—these are frustratingly familiar examples.

1. For these reasons I intend to discuss memory in what follows.

As you can see, the revised paragraph adds the kind of details and support that most readers appreciate. It not only gets to the point but also uses examples that readers can identify with.

Now that you see how to combine questioning with levels of generality, let's turn to some practice work. Below is a paragraph that follows the general/specific pattern. Using your own experience, write in appropriate details to support the paragraph's topic sentence.

EXERCISE 3.2: MEMORY
(Adding Details and Support)

1. Human memory can be astonishingly vivid.

   2. For example, as one hears a particular melody, long-forgotten memories may flood to mind.

3. For me, _____

_____

_____

_____

2. The same holds true for stimulation of the other senses—
for example, sight, touch, taste, and smell.

   3. When I see _____

_____

_____

_____

   3. When I touch [taste, smell] _____

_____

_____

_____

Details are the key to the general specific pattern. In this
case what matters are clear, relevant examples from personal
experience. Now compare your level-3 sentences with these:

> 3. For me, Elvis Presley tunes like "All Shook Up" and
> "Hound Dog" take me back many years—cruising down
> the boulevard in a '55 Ford pickup, with my elbow hooked
> out the window and my feet pounding to the Saturday-
> night beat.
>
> 3. When I see the leather-bound dictionary on my desk,
> I think of the neighborhood lady who gave me not only
> a treasured graduation gift but also a summer job, doing
> yard work for a dollar an hour. When I feel its frayed
> edges, I remember living at home my first year in college
> and trying to write papers for freshman classes that terri-
> fied me.

Notice that several parallel details would create a very
long paragraph. You'd then face the problem of dividing
this text into two smaller chunks. The logical place for such
a paragraph division, as you can probably see, is with the
second level-2 sentence.

The topic sentence you've been providing support for is *"Human memory can be astonishingly vivid."* But let's assume that you now want to shift gears, focusing your reader's attention on the *limitations* of memory. The pattern you'd use, of course, is compare-and-contrast order, in this case signaled with a contrast transition (*and yet*).

EXERCISE 3.3: MEMORY
(Adding Details and Support)

1. And yet _____

_____

2. I have trouble remembering _____

_____

_____

3. Recently, for example, _____

_____

_____

_____

_____

2. My memory seems particularly prone to fail when _____

_____

_____

_____

Try generating some sentences of your own, including a topic sentence at the top of the paragraph. Compare the sentences you create with ones written by other students.

CUTTING TO CLARIFY

As you learned in Chapter 2, it's sometimes tough to delete material. On the other hand, cutting away certain sentences—particularly irrelevant and redundant ones—can greatly improve the quality of your paragraphs. Careful reading precedes such surgery.

To practice cutting away unneeded material, identify the sentence in Exercise 3.4 that doesn't fit the general/specific order.

EXERCISE 3.4: MEMORY
(Cutting Unneeded Material)

1. Actually, information stored in human memory is never forgotten.

2. I spent a lot of time doing research in the library before I arrived at this conclusion.

2. Information remains with us for life unless erased by disease or injury.

2. This fact has been confirmed by researchers who map the brain's surface, applying mild electrical current at particular points.

3. Patients report minute details from experiences in the distant past—details, facts, and concepts seemingly long "forgotten."

In this exercise, you may notice how the focus shifts from the topic sentence to the writer's comment about working in the library, and then back to the topic, information. By cutting the sentence about library research, you eliminate the shift in focus and thus improve the paragraph.

Think of the next paragraph as an extension of the one

above; look for a single sentence that probably needs to be cut. You might note that this paragraph blends general/specific order, numerical order, and compare/contrast order.

EXERCISE 3.5: MEMORY
(Cutting Unneeded Material)

1. Thus, forgetting is not so much a *memory* problem as it is a problem of recalling.

2. I see two possible explanations for the problem of not being able to recall information from memory.

3. On the one hand, the data may be there but we can't find it.

4. This situation is familiar to anyone who has searched futilely through a filing cabinet (or a computer directory) for a known item.

3. On the other hand, the data may never have been transferred from short-term to long-term memory.

4. In this situation, the information is not available because it has never been filed.

2. Information stored in memory is never forgotten.

In this paragraph, the last sentence repeats the topic sentence from Exercise 3.4. Generally speaking, such redundancy weakens writing. Also, because this particular sentence doesn't really relate to the topic of recalling—the focus of this paragraph—it probably deserves to be cut.

REORGANIZING IN DEPTH

Let's now examine an exercise that uses three types of signals for its pattern of organization. Read the sentences carefully, thinking about how they might be reorganized. Watch for the cues associated with general/specific order, compare/contrast order, and numerical order. In reorganizing these sentences, find only the first *three* sentences and put them in the appropriate spaces below.

EXERCISE 3.6: MEMORY
(Reorganizing Practice)

A. Short-term memory (STM) is one system.

B. Human memory seems to consist of two systems.

C. The second remembering system is long-term memory (LTM).

D. Within STM there are actually two subsystems.

E. STM's second subsystem, working memory, is good for about thirty minutes.

F. LTM involves chemical changes in the brain.

G. One subsystem of STM, perceptual processing, lasts for a minute or less.

H. The capacity of LTM is unlimited because it is organized hierarchically—like Chinese boxes.

I. The capacity of STM is only about seven items.

J. LTM draws upon STM to create complex networks of knowledge.

1. ___

2. ___

3. ___

In Chapter 2 and in the first part of this chapter, you studied levels of generality, with numbers used to indicate levels. From this point on, we'll dispense with the numbers and use indentation to signal the levels of generality. The highest level of generality (level 1) will be set to the left; lower levels of generality (levels 2, 3, 4, etc.) will be indented.

Mathematically speaking, there are 3,628,000 possible combinations for reorganizing the ten exercise sentences, yet only a few combinations work for most readers. The odds are astronomically high that you opened your list with sentence B. Your sequence was probably B, A, C (plan 1 below) or B, A, D (plan 2 below).

 PLAN 1

Human memory seems to consist of two systems.

    Short-term memory (STM) is one system.

        The second remembering system is long-term memory (LTM).

 PLAN 2

Human memory seems to consist of two systems.

    Short-term memory (STM) is one system.

        Within STM there are actually two subsystems.

How could this be? How could your brain sort through millions of sentence sequences in just a few moments, fixing on one of these (or a slight variation) as its preferred pattern?

The answer is that your brain responds to certain cues that were built into the sentences. Among these cues were the general terms *human memory* and *two systems*. When you read through the sequence, you saw that all of the sentences pertained to memory; equally important, you noticed the division into two systems as an organizing pattern. The word *two* led you to notice related words (*one* and *second*) as well as the words *system* and *systems* in sentences B and C. You then faced the task of arranging the sentences logically.

Plan 1 announces two basic categories as its first move and then names them; next it deals with one category, short-term memory; and finally it presents the information on long-term memory. Plan 2 announces two categories and then deals immediately with the first category, short-term memory; this plan withholds sentence C (which introduces the category of long-term memory) until much later.

With one of these plans in mind, continue with your work of reorganizing sentences. You'll find it helpful to reread the exercise carefully as you rearrange its parts. Complete this task before reading on.

1. ____   6. ____

2. ____   7. ____

3. ____   8. ____

4. ____   9. ____

5. ____   10. ____

Let's now see how plan 1 and plan 2 for reorganizing the exercise sentences work themselves out. Your list may differ slightly from ones below, but it should be somewhat similar. Be prepared to discuss the plan (or pattern) that you prefer; that is, as a reader, do you prefer plan 1 (B, A, C, I, D, G, E, H, F, J) or plan 2 (B, A, D, G, E, I, C, J, F, H)?

PLAN 1

Human memory seems to consist of two systems.

Short-term memory (STM) is one system.

The second remembering system is long-term memory (LTM).

The capacity of STM is only about seven items.

Within STM there are actually two subsystems.

One subsystem, perceptual processing, lasts for a minute or less.

STM's second subsystem, working memory, is good for about thirty minutes.

The capacity of LTM is unlimited because it is organized hierarchically—like Chinese boxes.

LTM involves chemical changes in the brain.

LTM draws upon STM to create complex networks of knowledge.

 PLAN 2

Human memory seems to consist of two systems.

Short-term memory (STM) is one system.

Within STM there are actually two subsystems.

One subsystem of STM, perceptual processing, lasts for a minute or less.

STM's second subsystem, working memory, is good for about thirty minutes.

The capacity of STM is only about seven items.

The second remembering system is long-term memory (LTM).

LTM draws upon STM to create complex networks of knowledge.

LTM involves chemical changes in the brain.

The capacity of LTM is unlimited because it is organized hierarchically—like Chinese boxes.

In doing the exercise on human memory, you responded to cues in the sentences—words like *system, subsystem, STM,* and *LTM.* You were also trying to imagine how various sentences would fit together. Perhaps you wanted to change words or rearrange them slightly; or perhaps you felt the need for connectors to make smoother transitions.

Choosing a plan is difficult. After all, *both* plans organize sentences into easy-to-read chunks. Nevertheless, many readers seem to prefer plan 1. They say that the three opening sentences in plan 1 provide a kind of map for what follows. They like the predictability in structure. With plan 2, they say, more content must be held in mind. Which do you prefer?

MORE REORGANIZING PRACTICE

To apply what you've learned, read through the following set of disorganized sentences and find a logical order. (*Hint:* Look for numerical order as a paragraph pattern.) You'll find it helpful to circle the signal words in the sentences. Put the identifying letter for each sentence in the list following the exercise; then check your answers.

EXERCISE 3.7: MEMORY
(Reorganizing Practice)

A. Finally, LTM can be improved by relating new information to what we already know.

B. Because visualization organizes content by grouping, or *chunking,* ideas, it enhances the retrieval of information.

C. Simple verbal repetition, spaced over time, is one of the most basic, reliable methods.

D. A second LTM approach is to put information into visual patterns, diagrams, or pictures.

E. Reciting information aloud or processing it through writing seems to develop LTM traces.

F. Long-term memory (LTM) can be improved in three different ways.

G. The more we can "connect" old and new information, the more we will remember.

H. Using these three approaches, we can reduce the 80-percent forgetting rate that occurs in the first twenty-four hours following learning.

1. ____   5. ____

2. ____   6. ____

3. ____   7. ____

4. ____   8. ____

In addition to signal words such as numbers, you probably used other cues. For example, "verbal repetition" (sentence C) connects with "saying information aloud or processing it through writing" (sentence E). Similarly, "to put information into visual patterns, diagrams, or pictures" (sentence D) relates to "visualization" (sentence B). Most people who do this exercise organize the sentences like this: 1.F, 2.C, 3.E, 4.D, 5.B, 6.A, 7.G, 8.H.

PARAGRAPH PATTERNS REVISITED

To conclude this chapter, let's review the six basic patterns for paragraphs. We've focused on paragraph-level patterns because much revision occurs at this level. Also, by acquiring skill in paragraph revision, you develop an ability to work with longer stretches of text.

In what follows, each pattern is named and defined; then signal words that often accompany the pattern are listed. Study these patterns.

Spatial Order. Descriptive writing often presents sentences
that have physical location as an organizing scheme. You
use description when telling about an object, character's
appearance, or physical scene. The plan is often like a series
of snapshots, moving from left to right, from top to bottom,
or from near to far. Words and phrases that signal this pattern
include *above, below, beside, nearby, beyond, inside, outside,
across the hall, in the drawer,* and *toward the back.*

Time Order. Simple chronology (time order) is a basic
scheme for organizing sentences. You use time order whenever you narrate a story, but it is also used when explaining
a process—how to do or make something, for example, or
how something works. Words and phrases that signal this
pattern include *before, after, next, then, when, finally, while,
as, during, earlier, previously, later, thereupon, subsequently,
meanwhile,* and *as soon as.*

Numerical Order. Writing that explains often lists points
by number to assist the reader; and persuasive writing often
lists its points in order of increasing importance. Numerical
order is particularly useful when introducing, summarizing,
or classifying information. Words and phrases that signal
this pattern include numbers, of course, but also these: *one
factor, another type, also, finally, furthermore, moreover, in
addition, less powerful, equally important,* and *most significant.*

Cause/Effect Order. In dealing with causes, you specify *why*
something happened; in dealing with effects, you explain
the *results* of something. **Causes** pertain to events or conditions that are "behind" a certain situation; **effects** pertain
to events or conditions that "follow" from some situation.
Words and phrases that signal this pattern include *because,
since, for, in that, in order to, so, so that, as a result, therefore,
consequently, thus, hence, accordingly, the reason for,* and *the
reason why.*

Compare/Contrast Order. This pattern focuses on similarities and differences between objects, characters, scenes,
events, processes, or ideas. Either **comparisons** (likenesses)
or **contrasts** (differences) may be emphasized. As noted
above, comparison and contrast is sometimes teamed with

numerical order. Words and phrases that signal this pattern include the comparative and superlative forms of adjectives (*er/est; less/least; more/most*). Markers such as *also, additionally, just as, as if, as though, like, similarly,* and *in the same way* point to similarities while *but, yet, only, though, although, whereas, while, in contrast, conversely, still, however, on the other hand, rather, instead, in spite of, nevertheless,* and *on the contrary* point to differences.

General/Specific Order. This pattern, a staple of expository writing, consists of a general sentence plus more specific ones that provide examples, illustrations, or supporting detail. The general sentence names the topic and sometimes makes an assertion about it; the specific sentences reassert, amplify, or explain through instances. Although the general sentence usually comes early in the paragraph, it occasionally occurs last. Signal words and phrases—*such as, like, namely, more specifically, for example, for instance, to illustrate, that is, in fact, in other words,* and *indeed*—point to a narrower focus.

Look for these six patterns (and their combinations) when you revise. A search for paragraph patterns used will not only help you read your text at arm's length—from an imagined reader's viewpoint—but will also help you answer basic questions such as What works? What needs work?

Predictable text, with clear structure and a thoughtful treatment of the subject, can make reading a pleasure. On the other hand, when patterns are scrambled or somehow beyond us, we tend to give up. *Moral:* When meaning is missing, so is the reader.

LOOKING BACK, LOOKING AHEAD

In this chapter we have focused on adding, deleting, and reorganizing sentences. You have learned that each paragraph is a "chunk" of meaning, a way of "punctuating" the larger flow of text. You have seen that some paragraphs have distinctive patterns. Specifically, you have examined six patterns of organization and the words that signal these patterns.

The exercises that follow will provide practice in adding, cutting, and reorganizing sentences for clarity. Be on the lookout for places to use the transitions and signal words you learned because they can improve the structure of your prose by pointing the reader's attention. Also, some exercises may read well as unbroken chunks of text while others can be improved by paragraphing. Feel free to change or rearrange words or add connectors when doing these exercises. In Exercise 3.12, you'll apply skills of paragraph patterning to your own writing.

Chapter 4 builds on what you've learned here. You'll focus on finding links between sentences—a skill that can improve the coherence, or flow, of your writing. Such work will hone your surgical skills even further.

DO-IT-YOURSELF EXERCISES

Please be prepared to share your work in class. Your instructor will provide suggested answers for Exercises 3.8–3.11. Use Exercise 3.12 to make a personal application of paragraph patterns.

EXERCISE 3.8: NIGHT LIGHTS
(Adding Details and Support)

Directions: Revise the following paragraph by adding descriptive details in the blank spaces. Then circle the words that signal one or more of the following patterns:

Spatial order   Cause/effect order
Time order   Compare/contrast order
Numerical order   General/specific order

1. The view of the city was breathtaking.

2. Far below, traffic moved down dark canyons in a steady stream of light.

3. _____

_____

2. Farther out on the horizon, office buildings stood in glittering clusters.

3. _____

_____

2. Just beyond the downtown area, the lighted arch of a long bridge spanned the river's mouth.

3. _____

_____

2. And high above the scene was a slender crescent of moon in a cloudless sky.

3. _____

_____

EXERCISE 3.9: INTRODUCTION
(Cutting Unneeded Material)

Directions: Read the following introductory paragraph and check any sentences that probably should be deleted. Be prepared to support your decision for certain cuts in the paragraph. Then circle the words that signal one or more of the following patterns:

Spatial order	Cause/effect order
Time order	Compare/contrast order
Numerical order	General/specific order

1. My paper has several different aspects, which are quite fascinating.

2. In my opinion, it is important to cover the subject in a broad way and not get too technical or boring.

2. This paper has not been an easy one to write in many respects.

3. In fact, I have "sweated blood" over it, as the saying goes.

3. On the other hand, I have really learned a lot from it.

1. All in all, writing it has been an extremely worthwhile experience.

EXERCISE 3.10: SEX EDUCATION
(Reorganizing Practice)

Directions: Reorganize the following sentences by putting appropriate letters in the numbered blanks at the bottom of the exercise. Then circle the words that signal one or more of the following patterns:

Spatial order	Cause/effect order
Time order	Compare/contrast order
Numerical order	General/specific order

A. It is therefore not surprising that effective sex education in the home is lacking.

B. Many adult parents fear that sex education will encourage sexual activity.

C. Eighty percent of these teenage pregnancies result from premarital sex.

D. Presently, 10 percent of American women get pregnant by the age of 17, 25 percent by the age of 19.

E. Only 3 out of 10 teenagers aged 13 to 18 have had instruction about birth control in school.

F. Moreover, only about 30 percent of the nation's schools have sex education programs.

1. ____   4. ____

2. ____   5. ____

3. ____   6. ____

EXERCISE 3.11: CREATIVITY
(Reorganizing Practice)

Directions: Reorganize the following sentences by putting appropriate letters in the numbered blanks at the bottom of the exercise. Then circle the words that signal one or more of the following patterns:

Spatial order

Time order

Numerical order

Cause/effect order

Compare/contrast order

General/specific order

A. Mozart, for example, claimed to hear entire symphonies in his head before transcribing them.

B. Similarly, Edgar Allan Poe planned his stories with great precision and detail.

C. Like Beethoven, the novelist Dostoyevsky worked and reworked his art, wrestling with the emerging form.

D. Crossed-out lines in Beethoven's notebooks, for example, record the agony of countless false starts.

E. But for other artists, ideas emerge slowly and only after painful struggle.

F. Creative processes differ markedly among artists.

G. Some people carefully plan their creative work in advance.

H. These examples show clearly that "creativity" is more complex than we might at first suppose.

1. _____   5. _____

2. _____   6. _____

3. _____   7. _____

4. _____   8. _____

EXERCISE 3.12: PERSONAL APPLICATION

Practice in adding, cutting, and reorganizing sentences for clarity has introduced you to six patterns of organization: (1) time order, (2) spatial order, (3) numerical order, (4) compare/contrast order, (5) cause/effect order, and (6) general/specific order. These "plans" for organizing sometimes overlap.

To apply what you've learned about paragraph patterns, reread a completed paper or a draft of writing in progress. Find examples of at least two of these paragraph patterns in your own work. After finding these examples—even partial ones—photocopy the paragraphs.

Examine your paragraphs closely. Can they be strengthened by rearranging sentences? Is additional development needed? Has unneeded material been included? Make revision notes to improve both paragraphs; then do the actual rewriting. Reread the fresh copies of your revised paragraphs carefully.

Your task is to make a statement about your two paragraphs, using one of the six basic patterns. For example, you might use time order to narrate the process of revising. Or you might use numerical order to list the features that make one paragraph more readable than the other. Or you might use compare/contrast order to note the similarities or the differences between them. Or you might use general/specific order to discuss a writing principle, with supporting examples from the two paragraphs. The approach you take is up to you, but the content of your writing should be the two paragraphs you've revised.

Hand in your work from this application activity. Your packet of materials should contain the following: (1) photocopies of the original paragraphs, with revision notes, (2) your revisions of the two paragraphs, and (3) your follow-up writing about the paragraphs.

PROSE SURGERY IN ACTION

In this example of prose surgery, Keith Larsen compares and contrasts two of his college instructors. Notice that Keith's first draft begins slowly but that he adds details and support as the paper evolves. By describing the physical appearance of his professors, Keith creates a strong visual image that carries throughout his paper.

His changes are shown in one paragraph of Keith's conference draft; however, he made similar revisions elsewhere. Equally striking are revisions in the paper's organization. If you read the first two drafts carefully, you'll notice that the order in which the two teachers are presented isn't always consistent. Keith solved this problem in his final draft by making sure that he always dealt with his negative example first, his positive example second.

Notice, finally, Keith's skillful use of transitions—words and phrases like *both, also, likewise, in contrast, while, on the other hand, conversely,* and *however.* These transitions, when coupled with clear topic sentences and supporting details, help make the paper easy to follow and interesting to read.

Here are the four symbols used in class and in conferences to prompt revision and editing:

+ = I like this [word, phrase, sentence].

√ = Please check this [word, phrase, sentence].

? = I don't follow this [word, phrase, sentence].

= Think about developing this part more.

I Don't Like Statistics—or Do I?
(Response Draft)

I like to be taught by people who love what they do. For some reason their great enthusiasm at performing a certain activity rubs off on me and I become infected by the same desire to excell. Sometimes even a task that I don't care for at all becomes alive and fascinating to me when its shared with someone who takes great satisfaction in it. I also believe the opposite is true.

Teachers, by their classroom actions can either instill a love (or at least interest) in a subject or, conversely, bore you to tears, even if you liked that subject before.

I had an interesting experience that really brought this home to me once. I had signed up for statistics. I really didn't want to, but it was a required course, so I figured I just better get it over with. The same quarter I had gotten into the genetics class I needed and was really looking forward to it. *physical appearance*

Both teachers had extensive knowledge of the subject matter and were extremely intelligent. Also, they were both very organized in their presentation methods. The statistics teacher put his lecture on the chalkboard and the genetics teacher used overheads.

The problem with the overheads was a lot of them had been reproduced from a book. He described the overheads to a degree, but without the book they had come from as a reference, they made no sense. They came in boring succession, one after another as the teacher droned on from behind his beard in a deep monotone. The genetics professor was a brilliant man in his field, but this method of instruction failed to put the concepts across well.

On the other hand, the statistics teacher put a great deal of thought into whatever he told us. The lectures were simply put and very easy to understand. His notes seemed to <u>flow</u> <u>and walk</u> across the chalkboard in a precise and meaningful parade of concepts and ideas.

+ detail

+ transition

 # more detail

[*This draft goes on to compare and contrast the two instructors in broad, general terms.*]

I Don't Like Statistics—or Do I?

(Conference Draft)

Teachers, by their classroom actions can either instill love (or at least an interest) in a subject or, conversely, cause disinterest and boredom even if that subject was liked before. I had an experience that really brought this home to me. I had signed up for statistics. I didn't want to, but it was a required course, so I figured I had just better get it over with. The same

+ Clear opener

✓ Combine sentences

quarter I had gotten into the genetics class I needed and was really looking forward to it. ✓ *organization in relation to opening ¶.*

My genetics teacher had a thick brown beard that covered a good portion of his face. What wasn't masked by the beard was obscured by the shaded glasses he wore. He usually dressed *+detail* in earthy colors, mostly flannel shirts. All of this made him look very dark and mysterious, almost hidden, in fact. He was also very somber and dignified and had a deep mellow voice. *+ transition* My statistics teacher was, in contrast, a very classy dresser. He wore white pants and a colored shirt, kind of like the bright colored outfits you see in a Tide commercial. He had a very sharp, clean-shaven face with a strong jaw and a prominent *his* *+detail* pointed nose. His articulation was very clear and the New Zealand accent ~~he had~~ gave his words an interesting curl.

[*The above paper goes on to compare the intelligence and teaching approaches of the two instructors, focusing first on similarities, then on differences*]

What I Learned in Statistics

(and It Wasn't Statistics!)

by

Keith Larsen

Teachers, by their classroom actions, can either instill love (or at least an interest) in a subject or, conversely, cause disinterest and boredom even if that subject was liked before. For me, this point was driven home during the term I took genetics, a class I was looking forward to, and statistics, a class I had to take although I didn't want to.

My genetics teacher had a thick brown beard that covered a good portion of his face. What wasn't masked by the beard was obscured by the shaded glasses he wore. He usually dressed in earthy colors, mostly flannel shirts and polyester slacks. All of this made him look very dark and mysterious, almost hidden, in fact. He was also very somber and dignified, with a deep mellow voice. My statistics teacher, in contrast, was a very classy dresser. He wore white pants and a colored shirt, like the bright-colored outfits you see in a Tide commercial. He had a very sharp, clean-shaven face with a strong jaw and a prominent, pointed nose. His articulation was very clear, and his New Zealand accent gave his words an interesting curl.

Both teachers had an extensive knowledge of their respective subjects and were extremely intelligent. My genetics teacher had been taught by some of the great names in genetics research. He knew some of the scientists mentioned in our textbook personally. He did most of the problems associated with the classwork in his head as he explained them. Likewise, the statistics teacher knew the men who had written the text we used and was in frequent contact with them, offering his insights for improvements. He would also do some pretty fast calculations in his head, usually as quick as I could punch them out on my calculator.

While both teachers were very organized in their presentations, it soon became apparent how different their methods were. The genetics teacher used overheads. They were all neatly placed in a green folder and put in order in his filing cabinet.

All he did was pull that day's file and bring it to class, put it in front of him on the table, and slowly roll each overhead onto the projector. The problem was that most of the overheads had been reproduced from a book. They came in boring succession, one after another, as he droned on.

On the other hand, the statistics professor put a great deal of thought into whatever he told us. He brought his notes on yellow sheets of paper and transferred them to the chalkboard. Everything on the board flowed smoothly from one concept to another. There were no distractions, and everything had a reason for being there. He put ideas so clearly and simply that he was very easy to follow.

In genetics, when a student didn't understand a point and asked a question, it was greeted with an impatient stare and the same example or point was merely repeated. When the same concept was questioned again, the professor would raise his voice and bellow, "Come on, people!" Then he would repeat the point while his tone of voice betrayed his impatience. I never wanted to ask a question because he always made me feel stupid.

Conversely, questions in statistics elicited comments of "thank you" or "good question" and a clear answer. It was easy to ask questions and interact with our statistics professor because he made our questions seem important and valid. Each question was treated with enthusiasm.

The genetics teacher rarely had more than one example per concept. The professor never showed us how problems could be asked in a different way or with different variables, even if we asked. We were left to chip away at our teacher's hardened outer crust and try to find out on our own just exactly what he wanted from us. Also, the problems in lectures and the ones on the tests did not correspond to one another.

My statistics teacher, however, gave many different examples. His examples really applied to what we were doing. He would always tell us how to interpret the scientific research that we saw on television. In fact, he made us see research in a whole different light. He also showed many new angles from which to approach problems. The homework, lectures, and tests always had the same type of problems. If it was in a lecture, we could expect a similar problem on the test.

At the beginning of the quarter I had expected to enjoy genetics and be bored to tears in statistics. However, it actually turned out the other way. Genetics became as dead as the teacher's lectures, and statistics became interesting. The reason for this was that statistics permeated everything my teacher did. He actually enjoyed figuring out means and standard deviations using our test scores. Teaching excited him. He gave the subject life and helped me get the best grade I had ever gotten in a math class.

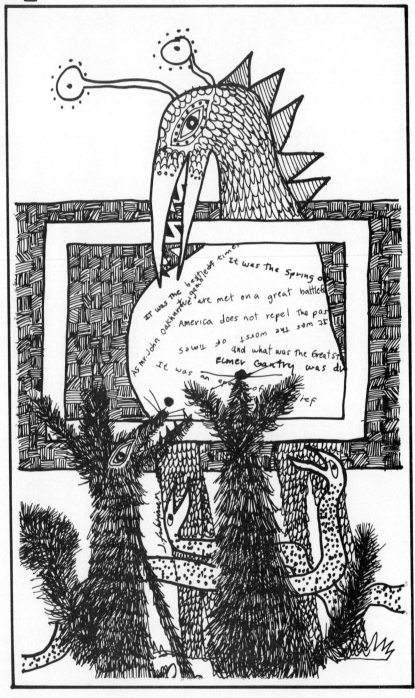

READING TO EDIT: SEEING SENTENCE CONNECTIONS

A good surgeon must have an eagle's eye, a lion's heart, and a lady's hand.

—PROVERB

Scene: You and your writing instructor in the hallway after class.

"So how's the editing coming?"

"I don't know. My paper's organized, I think, but something's not right. The sentences don't flow. I mean, I read over my paragraphs and—well, it's hard to describe—"

"Sort of zigzag? Choppy?"

"Yeah, like some of the sentences don't really connect, you know? I mean, they're on the same topic and all. And I've done lots of revising to develop support. But something's missing."

Your instructor shrugs. "Welcome to the club. I know just what you mean."

"You do?"

"Sure. You've got all these threads of meaning—these individual sentences and paragraphs—but they're not sticking together the way you hoped. It happens all the time—to everybody who cares about their writing."

"Not sticking together—that describes it."

"It's what textbooks call a 'coherence problem'."

"So what does that mean?"

"*Coherence?* The word is derived from Latin. It means 'clinging together'."

"Yeah, but what's the problem?"

"Well, think of yourself as a spider trying to spin a web," your instructor says. "You've got these lovely silken threads of words, but they're separate, unconnected. The problem you face is getting them to stick together at the right places to create a web of meaning."

"Hmmmmm. 'A web of meaning.' You mean something that makes sense, right?"

"Sure—making sense is the whole point of writing."

"So how do I do that?"

"Do what?"

"Get sentences and paragraphs to stick together."

"By doing what you're doing."

"Which is?"

"Questioning the text like you're questioning me."

"That's all there is to it?"

"That's a lot."

CHAPTER PREVIEW

This chapter explores the "web of meaning" from the inside out. It shows how words point to one another, creating **ties** (or links) across sentence and paragraph boundaries. What it says about pointing will help you question your text and edit it.

Think about the x-rays that dentists, physicians, and scientists use to see into various structures, including the human body. We'll use a kind of mental x-ray to see cohesive links between various interconnecting sentences. Your hunches about "what makes sense" provide the energy source for this probing of beneath-the-surface structure.

When you check coherence, you ask yourself, To what extent do these sentences connect? But answering this question isn't like math, where right (or wrong) answers reward your efforts. Instead, you must read and reread for meaning, fingering and adjusting the threads of words.

Exercises in this unit, which use the x-ray idea, are designed to help you diagnose how well sentences cohere in illustrative paragraphs. However, learning about sentence-to-sentence coherence will also help you understand coherence between paragraphs.

DIAGNOSING COHERENCE

In reading the two paragraphs that follow, you'll notice a striking difference in coherence.

 TEXT 1

A. Writing well is a complex intellectual task.

B. It first requires considerable creativity and risktaking.

C. In other words, good writers have the courage to follow unplanned, imaginative impulses.

D. But successful writing also demands tough-minded discipline.

E. It requires one to work in a steady, thoughtful way.

 TEXT 2

A. Writing well is a complex intellectual task.

B. A task may be done either inside or outside.

C. Outside storm windows can significantly reduce heating bills, particularly in cold weather.

D. Weather satellites now track storm patterns, providing data for predictions.

E. Predictions made by the chair of the Federal Reserve may affect stock prices dramatically.

The two passages start out with the same sentence. But only text 1 hangs together and makes sense. Text 2 begins to unravel at sentence B, and the coherence worsens as you read on. After reading the last sentence in text 2, you may well have begun *rereading*, trying to make sense of nonsense: "What does the Federal Reserve have to do with writing well?" If you diagnosed text 2 as lacking coherence, you're correct.

Examine text 1 again and you will see that all its sentences point back to the same topic—namely, the idea of writing well. This paragraph explains that writing well has two sides to it. In text 2, however, something is wrong. Each sentence in text 2 uses a single word from the prior sentence (*task, outside, weather, predictions*) to point ahead to a new, unrelated topic. So this paragraph explains nothing, except perhaps how to confuse a reader. Although the sentences in text 1 can be rearranged and still make sense, no amount of reorganizing will improve text 2.

From text 1 we see that sentences must have a shared topic if they are to make sense as a paragraph. This is probably an obvious point, but it's an important one as you begin to diagnose writing problems at the paragraph level. Without a shared topic, sentences don't hang together. In addition, sentences must point to words (or ideas) within each other, not to words or ideas outside the topic frame of the paragraph.

THREE TYPES OF COHESIVE LINKS

Sentences must be on the same topic for coherence to occur; but merely having a set of sentences on the same topic does not necessarily make for good writing. There are three main ways to connect sentences.

Grammar Links. Pronouns such as *this, these, that, he, she, it, they, some, one* point across sentence boundaries to link sentences together.

Vocabulary Links. Repeated words, synonyms, antonyms, and words in the same "family of meaning" point across sentence boundaries to link sentences together.

Transition Links. Signal words and phrases such as *but, however, also, moreover, in addition, for example, therefore, in conclusion* point across sentence boundaries to link sentences together.

We can indicate the direction of cohesive links with arrows. A backward-pointing link (by far the most common kind of sentence-to-sentence cohesion) is indicated with [←——]. Predictably, a forward-pointing link is indicated with [——→], and a transition link is indicated with [←—→].

To illustrate each of these links briefly, here are three pairs of sentences. Each x-ray shows the link being discussed.

 X-RAY 1: GRAMMAR LINKS

A. Grammar links help with cohesion.

Sentence A   **Sentence B**

grammar links   ←——   they

B. Often they are pronouns that refer to nouns in preceding sentences.

 X-RAY 2: VOCABULARY LINKS

C. Vocabulary links also create cohesion.

Sentence C		Sentence D
vocabulary links	←———	repeated [words]
vocabulary links	←———	related words
cohesion	←———	hang together

D. Repeated and related words help sentences hang together.

X-RAY 3: TRANSITION LINKS

E. Finally, transition links help sentences to cohere.

Sentence D	←(finally)→	Sentence E
Sentence E	←(for example)→	Sentence F

F. For example, signal words may be used to connect sentences.

The most basic fact of sentence-to-sentence cohesion, as you can see, is that links occur in pairs. An item in one sentence points to an item in another sentence. In the process of reading, we make connections between and among these words; this connection is part of what we call **coherence** (or the "flow" of writing).

Notice that most links point *back* to a word or phrase in the previous sentence. With transition links, the arrows point *both* ways. Later you will see that some links point *ahead* to sentences that follow; however, these forward-pointing links occur only occasionally in written English.

COHESION IN A PARAGRAPH

For a slightly more complex example of cohesion at work, let's look carefully at text 1, which opened this chapter. This x-ray analysis shows the key links, not the subtler ones. Once again, it illustrates how links point across sentence boundaries.

 TEXT 1

A. Writing well is a complex intellectual task.

B. It first requires considerable creativity and risktaking.

C. In other words, good writers have the courage to follow unplanned, imaginative impulses.

D. But successful writing also demands tough-minded discipline.

E. It requires one to work in a steady, thoughtful way.

COHESION X-RAY

Sentence A	←(first)→	Sentence B
writing well	←——	it
complex task	←——	creativity
complex task	←——	risktaking

Sentence B	←(in other words)→	Sentence C
risktaking	←——	courage
creativity	←——	unplanned [impulses]
creativity	←——	imaginative impulses

Sentence C	←(but)→	Sentence D
Sentence C	←(also)→	Sentence D
good writers	←——	successful writing

Sentence D		Sentence E
successful writing	←———	it
discipline	←———	work
discipline	←———	steady
tough-minded	←———	thoughtful

An example of a grammar link occurs between sentences A and B. Notice that *it* refers to *writing well*. A second example of a grammar link occurs between sentences D and E, where *it* points to *successful writing*. For the word *it* to make sense in both cases, a reader must find the word (or phrase) to which *it* refers. This process creates cohesion between the sentences.

There are many examples of vocabulary links in the preceding x-ray. Between sentences B and C, for example, *courage* points to *risktaking*. Why? Because we think of courage as involving risks. In similar fashion, the phrase *unplanned, imaginative impulses* points to *creativity*. Actually, each of these words is an aspect of creativity. Some vocabulary links are created by repeated words, others by synonyms or near-synonyms, and still others by words in the same "family of meaning." Notice, for example, that *work* refers to *discipline*. In terms of meaning, these words are in the same "family."

Finally, notice that *signal words* in parentheses—the transition links—connect entire sentences, not just individual words. Transitions serve as signposts for the reader, helping to reveal the structure of the paragraph. These signposts point both backward and forward in the text.

After studying the cohesion x-ray for a few moments, reread text 1. Pay attention to where you must refer to make sense of specific words. As you do this, you'll catch glimmers of beneath-the-surface ties, the links we have just studied. From this brief demonstration, you can probably see how important such links are for writing quality. Writing that coheres generally has a network of ties between and among sentences.

Cohesive links can be **immediate** (close together), **chained** (occurring in more than one sentence), or **remote** (separated by one or more sentences). As you might guess, good writing has a higher percentage of immediate and chained links than does ineffective writing.

To summarize, here are some points to remember about coherence in prose:

1. Most links point *back* to a preceding word or idea.

2. A few point *ahead* to words that follow.

3. Some point *both* ways, joining two sentences.

By focusing on the types of cohesion and their direction, you begin to "see" the structure of prose.

MAKING COHESION X-RAYS

To practice spotting cohesive links, read the accompanying paragraph and then fill in words on the x-ray answer sheet. Afterward, check your work against the answers that follow.

EXERCISE 4.1: TWO HEMISPHERES
(Checking Coherence)

A. For most people, the left hemisphere of the brain is analytic.

B. It prefers logic, order, and step-by-step sequences.

C. This side specializes in language and mathematics.

D. The right hemisphere, however, is synthetic and creative.

E. It likes global design, visual imagery, rhythm, and metaphor.

F. This side enjoys subjects such as art and music.

G. Writing is one activity that integrates both the left and right hemispheres.

Sentence A		Sentence B
left hemisphere	←———	———————
analytic	←———	———————
analytic	←———	———————
analytic	←———	———————

Sentence B		Sentence C
it [left hemisphere]	←———	———————

Sentence C	←(___)→	Sentence D
this side	←———	———————

Sentence D		Sentence E
right hemisphere	←———	———————
synthetic and creative	←———	———————
synthetic and creative	←———	———————
synthetic and creative	←———	———————
synthetic and creative	←———	———————

Sentence E		Sentence F
it [right hemisphere]	←———	———————
global design	←———	———————
rhythm	←———	———————

Now compare your answers with these: (sentence B) it, logic, order, step-by-step sequences; (sentence C) this side; (sentence D) however, the right hemisphere; (sentence E) it, global design, visual imagery, rhythm, metaphor; (sentence F) this side, art, music.

As you may have noticed, this x-ray leaves out a number of links that are "chained" through the paragraph. For example, sentences A and D are linked; so are sentences B and E as well as C and F. These sentences, linked by the word *however*, contrast with each other.

Notice, too, that the final sentence of the paragraph is not part of the x-ray. Sentence G links back to sentences A and D, which make statements about the hemispheres of the brain. You could even make the case that sentence G is linked to *all* of the sentences that precede it.

The "exceptions" noted above serve to emphasize that analyzing cohesion is hardly an exact science—nor should it be, for our purposes. Exactness isn't the issue in diagnosing how well a text hangs together. The point is to have a rough idea of possible trouble spots *before* beginning to edit. Such a diagnosis makes the time you spend in prose surgery more productive than it might otherwise be.

For the same kind of analytic practice, but focusing on the left rather than the right column, go to work on the following paragraph. After filling in the left column, check your work against the answers that follow.

EXERCISE 4.2: FAD DIETS
(Checking Coherence)

A. Each month a new fad diet hits the bookstores.

B. For all of their differences, these diets have one thing in common.

C. They promise a slim body with virtually no effort.

D. Each diet "documents" its claims with testimonials from people who magically transformed their waistlines, not to mention their lives, in just a week or two.

E. The jackets advertise a better life on one condition.

F. The individual must make a "Commitment to the Program."

G. That "commitment" begins, of course, with the price of the book.

Sentence A   **Sentence B**

_____   ⟵   these diets

Sentence B		Sentence C
_____	⟶	they
_____	⟵	promise

Sentence C		Sentence D
_____	⟵	each diet
_____	⟵	magically
_____	⟵	waistlines

Sentence D		Sentence E
_____	⟵	jackets
_____	⟵	life

Sentence E		Sentence F
_____	⟶	all of sentence F

Sentence F		Sentence G
_____	⟵	"commitment"
_____	⟵	begins

Now compare your answers with these: (sentence A) fad diet; (sentence B) these diets, thing in common; (sentence C) they [the diets], no effort, slim body; (sentence D) diet, lives; (sentence E) one condition; (sentence F) Commitment, make.

You should note in the preceding x-ray that two of the links point *ahead*, to sentences that follow. Between sentences B and C, for example, is a forward-pointing link. Sentence C tells what the diets have in common. A similar kind of link occurs between sentences E and F. Sentence F gives the one condition for a better life.

Forward-pointing links are often signaled by one of two punctuation marks—the colon and the dash. Putting colons between each of the sentence pairs above would strengthen their cohesion. Why? Because a colon tells the reader that what follows is closely related to what has gone before.

MORE COMPLEX COHESION

Finally, let's look at a longer paragraph, one with a more complex network of cohesive links. Here you will find subtle vocabulary links in addition to obvious grammar links. After reading the paragraph carefully, ask yourself, What is the main way that sentences are linked together? What words recur in difference sentences, helping to "chain" the text together? Take your time, and fill in both sides of this x-ray sentence.

EXERCISE 4.3: FIRST DAY OF CLASS
(Checking Coherence)

A. On the first day of class, students stake out the desks that they will occupy for several weeks.

B. If the class is important or likely to be difficult, they usually try to sit up close.

C. Otherwise, they aim for midrange or remote seating.

D. Their angle on the instructor presents a second decision.

E. Most students seem uncomfortable when seated directly in front of the instructor.

F. Perhaps they are nervous about being called on when unprepared.

G. Perhaps they worry about the problem of maintaining eye contact.

H. Whatever the reason, students often aim for seating at the periphery of the room.

I. This vantage point may enable them to be partially detached spectators rather than engaged participants.

Sentence A

——————
——————
——————

←——————
←——————
←——————

Sentence B

——————
——————
——————

Sentence B

←(———)→

——————
——————
——————

←——————
←——————
←——————

Sentence C

——————
——————
——————

Sentence C

——————

←——————

Sentence D

——————

Sentence D

——————
——————

←——————
←——————

Sentence E

——————

Sentence E

——————
——————
——————

←——————
←——————
←——————

Sentence F

——————
——————
——————

Sentence F

——————
——————
——————

←——————
←——————
←——————

Sentence G

——————
——————
——————

Sentence G

——————

←——————

Sentence H

——————

Sentence H

——————
——————

←——————
←——————

Sentence I

——————
——————

Now compare your pairs of links with these: (sentences A/B) class←——class; students←——they; desk←——sit; (sentences B/C) they [students]←——they [students]; sit←——seating; up close←——midrange or remote; (sentences C/D) they [students]←——their [the students]; (sentences D/E) angle ←——in front of; decision [for students]←——most students; (sentences E/F) students←——they [students]; uncomfortable ←——nervous; instructor←——called on [by instructor]; (sentences F/G) perhaps←——perhaps; they [students]←——they [students]; nervous←——worry; (sentences G/H) they [students]←——students; (sentences H/I) seating at periphery ←——this vantage point; students←——them.

As you probably noticed, pronouns such as *they, their,* and *them* connect to the word *students.* These pronouns, plus the repetition of the word *students,* provide the main source of connectedness for the paragraph. But notice also that other words—*class, desk,* and *instructor*—are in the same "family of meaning" as *students.* Each of these words, in turn, has its own network of connections.

Two subtle transitions are not included in the x-ray. Look back at sentence D to spot the phrase *second decision.* No mention has been made of a *first decision* in the earlier sentences, though that is implied. Another transition link occurs in sentence H, with the phrase *whatever the reason* [for their discomfort]. This phrase refers to two hypothetical reasons that precede sentence H; yet these sentences (F and G) do not announce themselves as reasons. Notice, finally, that many links point back through several preceding sentences.

No one expects you to make such sentence-by-sentence x-rays when you edit your own paragraphs. The purpose here has been to show you how cohesion works. Simply paying attention to cohesion will help you reread your own writing for sentence-to-sentence connections; it is such reading that helps you engage in careful editing.

MAKING SENSE OF COHERENCE

To conclude this chapter, let's consider coherence from the inside out. How can we do this? By watching how you read the next few paragraphs and thinking about what happens.

Glancing ahead just now, you see paragraphs in this section as "chunks" of text. To *read* them, however, you must follow a thread of words left-to-right-and-down-the-page. You're really unaware of this "tracking" process. As you read, however, a fair number of your brain's 30 billion neurons will go to work, weaving a web of meaning within you.

Notice, as you read this third paragraph, how you are pulled along. The back-and-forth sweep of your eyes is relentless, voracious. Pay attention as your eyes leap ahead for a split second. Now they pause. And in this instant— the one right now—they follow the thread of words further, wending their way through neat, parallel rows of black on white, taking in phrase after phrase—then pausing again before making the leap across white space to the next paragraph.

So far, so good. Now pause to consider the web of meaning you've been spinning. You see the words, but you cannot see their meaning. Why? Because meaning exists *inside* you. Meaning is something you "hear" or "feel" more than something you see. It's what you, the reader, spin for yourself by connecting words and sentences with past learning.

Thus the thread of words—these words—moves you down the page. But unless you're able to spin a web of personal meaning while reading the words, the writing will fail to make sense. The cohesiveness of the writing increases the likelihood that you will spin a web of meaning. The way that sentence threads are woven together, whether tightly or loosely, makes up its **cohesion;** and the points of connection among the interwoven sentences are its cohesive links. Cohesion depends on some kind of *relation* between two or more words in different sentences (or, sometimes, in different parts of the same sentence).

And how important are these links? Researchers have compared high-rated and low-rated student essays with regard to cohesion. They have learned that skilled writers use many more cohesive links—and many more types of links—than do less-skilled writers. The implication is clear: You can markedly improve the quality of your writing by paying attention to cohesive links—the "connectedness" of your ideas.

LOOKING BACK, LOOKING AHEAD

This chapter has focused on the editing skill of finding cohesive links between and among sentences. As you saw, there are three main ways to connect sentences: grammar links, vocabulary links, and transition links. Most links point *back* to the words in prior sentences; however, some links point *ahead*, often signaled by colons and dashes, and transition links point *both* ways.

The exercises that follow will help you look for cohesive ties in your own writing. If you find cohesive breaks in your text, you'll need to check whether pronouns and their antecedents are clearly (and correctly) connected, whether key words point across sentence boundaries, and whether appropriate transitions are used. Making connections more explicit is the typical editing approach.

In Chapter 5, the focus shifts to editing in a more conventional sense—namely, trimming flabby sentences. This is prose surgery that improves the "look" of your sentences once the cohesive ties are clear and explicit. The chapter builds on what you've learned here.

DO-IT-YOURSELF EXERCISES

Please be prepared to share your work in class. Your instructor will provide suggested answers for Exercises 4.4–4.7. Use Exercise 4.8 to make a personal application of editing for coherence.

EXERCISE 4.4: THE OFFICE
(Checking Coherence)

A. With papers and boxes stacked everywhere, the office was a mess.

Sentence A		Sentence B
office	←——	it
office	←——	room
mess	←——	clutter

B. It was a small room, made smaller by clutter and the smell of dusty books.

Sentence B		Sentence C
it [office]	←——	_____
it [office]	←——	_____
clutter	←——	_____

C. The desk chair and the typewriter were heaped with paper debris.

Sentence C		Sentence D
desk chair	←——	_____
debris	←——	_____

D. A few Styrofoam cups, their insides crusted with stale coffee, stood sentry on a desk top strewn with unfinished work.

Sentence D		Sentence E
unfinished work	←——	_____

E. Out-of-date memos, news clippings, and scrawled notes had been taped to the walls and stuck to the bulletin board.

Sentence E		Sentence F
scrawled notes	←———	——————

F. One ironic inscription, neatly lettered in calligraphy, read "Everything in Its Place."

EXERCISE 4.5: ONE CLOSE SHAVE
(Checking Coherence)

A. Nick searched the medicine cabinet for an aerosol can and then closed the mirror door.

Sentence A		Sentence B
Nick	←———	his palm
aerosol can	←———	shaving cream

B. White shaving cream billowed across his palm like a thunderhead.

Sentence B		Sentence C
——————	←———	lather
——————	←———	his chin and jawbones
——————	←———	he

C. Smearing lather under his chin and over his jawbones, he then reached for a long-handled tool.

Sentence E		Sentence D
——————	←———	razor
——————	←———	foam

D. The razor sliced a pass through the foam, scraping one cheek, then the other.

Sentence D	Sentence E
_____	← he
_____	← shave
_____	← chin

E. As he started to shave his chin, he saw a bright film of blood.

Sentence E	Sentence F
_____	← he
_____	← nicked
_____	← once again

F. He nicked his chin once again before he was finished and then splashed his face with cold water, ready to face a new day.

EXERCISE 4.6: AN INTELLIGENT DIET
(Checking Coherence)

A. An intelligent diet is like an insurance policy that minimizes future risks.

Sentence A	Sentence B
diet	← such a diet
diet	← animal fats
diet	← cholesterol

B. Such a diet is low in animal fats and cholesterol because these are associated with heart disease, our nation's number-one killer.

Sentence B		Sentence C
diet	←——	————
————	←——	————
————	←——	————
our nation	←——	————

C. Its goal is to reduce cholesterol to levels like those in societies where people rarely get heart disease.

Sentence C		Sentence D
its goal	←——	————

D. This diet does not include egg yolks, hot dogs, shrimp, or dairy products like butter and ice cream.

Sentence D		Sentence E
————	←——	excluded

Note: ←(___)→ between Sentence D and Sentence E

E. Also excluded are cheeseburgers, French fries, and pizzas.

Sentence E		Sentence F
excluded	←——	————

F. Lean meat, fish, and fowl are allowed, but the servings are modest—about 10 ounces per day.

Sentence F		Sentence G
diet [sentences A/B/D]←——		————

G. The diet is high in vegetables, cereals and breads, and fruits.

Sentence G		Sentence H
————	←——	————

Note: ←(___)→ between Sentence G and Sentence H

H. Moreover, it includes skim milk, vegetable oils with no cholesterol, and unsalted nuts.

EXERCISE 4.7: ALCOHOL ADVERTISING
(Checking Coherence)

A. Ads for alcohol make drinking seem glamorous.

Sentence A   **Sentence B**

seem glamorous   ⟵——   this [fact]

B. The reason for this is easy to understand:

Sentence B   **Sentence C**

_____   ——⟶   _____

C. Advertisers know that 93 percent of the alcohol sold is consumed by a mere 23 percent of the people who drink.

Sentence C   ⟵(___)⟶   **Sentence D**

_____   ⟵——   _____

_____   ⟵——   _____

D. Thus a select group of heavy drinkers is the target of their appeal.

Sentence D   **Sentence E**

_____   ⟵——   _____

_____   ⟵——   _____

E. Their basic pitch is that daily drinking is normal and that drinking makes life more pleasurable.

Sentence E   Sentence F

_____   ←——   _____

_____   ←——   _____

F. Watching these ads leads us to believe that those who drink are "with it"—socially and sexually.

Sentence F   ←(____)→   Sentence G

_____   ←——   _____

_____   ←——   _____

G. For example, beer commercials regularly portray the camaraderie of "macho types" enjoying each other's company.

Sentence G   Sentence H

_____   ←——   _____

_____   ←——   _____

H. In other commercials, we see slim-hipped young men and women flirting with one another as background music pulses.

EXERCISE 4.8: PERSONAL APPLICATION

This chapter has introduced you to three main ways to connect sentences: (1) grammar links, (2) vocabulary links, and (3) transition links. In this application exercise, you'll look for such links in your own prose. This work will help set the stage for editing.

Find two connected paragraphs in a paper you've already written or are now revising. These paragraphs should be ones that you regard as examples of strong cohesion. After finding these examples, look for another brief section of similar length that seems to have problems. This second sample may come from a paper that your instructor has already evaluated. Photocopy the "strong" and "problem" sections of text and label them as such.

Now make a close analysis of the links between sentences (and paragraphs) in the two samples. Underline the words in each sample that seem to make cohesive ties. With the underlining completed, go back to each sample and count the total number of ties. Finally, divide the total number of ties in each section by the total number of words. You will come up with a percentage figure—the ratio of cohesive ties to total words—for both your "strong" and "problem" texts. How do these percentages compare? Do they confirm your intuitions? Write a paragraph about your observations and conclusions.

Turn back to your "problem" text. What can you do to improve it? Read your text sentence by sentence. Now, on a clean sheet of paper, rewrite the problem paragraphs, inserting appropriate links and changing the wording to create stronger links. When you're satisfied with your work, once again underline the links, count them, and divide by the total number of words in the section. How does this percentage compare with the two computed earlier? What have you learned from this analysis? Write a second paragraph dealing with these questions.

Hand in your work from this application activity. Your packet of materials should contain the following: (1) labeled photocopies of the original paragraphs, with underlined cohesive ties; (2) your computation of percentages (ratios of cohesive ties to total words) for both "strong" and "problem" text samples; (3) a revision of your "problem" text, with emphasis on stronger cohesive links; and (4) two paragraphs of follow-up writing that deal with your observations and conclusions regarding both your original and your rewritten paragraphs.

PROSE SURGERY IN ACTION

Finding an opening that *feels* right—and sets a good direction for your essay—is a personal matter. Julianne Bales knew that the early draft of her case study on literacy learning wasn't quite right. So, rather than tinker with the wording, she made a fresh start, introducing the subject—her son, Brandon—with her first sentence.

How did Julianne make this decision? Reading aloud, she felt that her rough draft was "flat"—that it *told* about Brandon but *showed* very little. By choosing to use her real day-to-day interaction with Brandon as a point of departure, she found a way *into* her essay. This decision helped give her writing immediacy and voice.

As her essay began to take shape, Julianne made other important revising and editing decisions. For her response draft, for example, she was able to complete only about 400 words before she was scheduled to meet with her response group. Instead of skipping class, she made notes at the end of the draft—a smart strategy. This planning helped with the flow of her writing.

Notice how Julianne uses time-order words and phrases— *after, while, later,* and so on—to connect her sentences and paragraphs. Notice, too, how she uses a variety of grammar links, vocabulary links, and transition links to help her sentences and paragraphs hang together.

Here are the four symbols used in class and in conferences to prompt revision and editing:

+ = I like this [word, phrase, sentence].

√ = Please check this [word, phrase, sentence].

? = I don't follow this [word, phrase, sentence].

= Think about developing this part more.

Untitled

(Rough Draft)

Sitting back in the soft corner of the sofa, I gazed up at the three pictures on my fireplace mantel. Those of my children, two sons and a daughter.

Brandon is the oldest, he is eight years old and in the second grade. Michael is the middle child and just turned 5 and Brooke is only eight months old. I selected Brandon for my subject in a study of literacy. As a first born, he has been a victim of trial and error on many accounts, and my insight on his state of literacy and study into his negative and positive experiences could help me as his parent make changes necessary to enhance his future learning and that of his younger brother and sister also.

Brandon is a very social child. He likes to have lots of friends. At this point in his life, it is important to be "rad." He likes his hair spiked on top and spends quite a lot of time getting it just right in the bathroom. He likes bugle boy pants and Air Jordan high top gym shoes.

[*This draft ends without further development.*]

Untitled
[Response Draft]

[*From a section near the end of the response draft.*]

Brandon's father is very active in sports and it is not a coincidence that Brandon finds sports appealing also. Being the first boy, Brandon has to cope with his father's expectations of him as an athlete. But, even with this full schedule he can't resist playing with his baby sister, Brooke, or Nintento with Michael. . . .

I asked Brandon if he enjoyed t̶o̶ r̶e̶a̶d̶. *reading* "No! It's boring!" he answered. I asked him if it would help to go to the library *⁺dialogue* and get some "new" books. He nodded with approval ✓and we made plans to go the next day.

   The Library Event

      What kind of books interest him?

      Did he spend more time doing homework?   *+ planning*

      Was he more interested?

   A Writing Test

      Does he like to write?

      Have him write a letter to grandmother.

      Have him write me a story.

Putting Meaning Behind Learning
by
Julianne Bales

My computer screen was blank and so was my mind until Brandon, my son, came in from the dark hallway, bringing with him many ideas for my case study on literacy. Brandon has often come into the room where my computer sits and watched me work. On this morning when he asked his usual question--"What are you working on?"--I replied with a quite definite answer: "I think I will write a paper on you!"

   Brandon was surprised. His eyebrows raised, and his green eyes widened with excitement. "No! I don't want anyone reading about me!" he exclaimed. Brandon has been very curious about my college life, and we have discussed on many occasions the events that take place--including peer response groups. His eyes sparkled as he danced out of the room to finish getting ready for school.

After taking great care in his dress and appearance, Brandon joined his younger brother, Michael (5 years old), at the break-fast table. Brandon was wearing his acid-washed Levis and his favorite oversized, blue and grey sweatshirt. His hair was carefully spiked on the top of his head and he wore a fluorescent green and black striped friendship bracelet on his wrist. Bran-don's father has teased him on several occasions about wearing a "girl's" bracelet, but Brandon defended his position each time by explaining that it is "rad" and that all the "cool" guys wear them.

While fixing breakfast for the boys, I explained to Brandon that I would need to interview him after school for my paper. He chuckled. "You can't! I have scouts after school today." At 8 years of age, Brandon is a very busy second grader. He has scouts on Wednesdays, wrestling on Thursdays, and will soon be starting soccer. In addition to these activities, he must do twenty-five minutes of homework each evening--twenty min-utes of reading and five minutes of spelling or math. When Brandon isn't engaged in one of those activities, you can find him playing "peek-a-boo" with his baby sister, Brook (9 months old), or "Teenage Mutant Ninja Turtles" (a video game) on the Nintendo with Michael.

Later that day, after Brandon's scout meeting, Brandon and I sat down together to do our homework. Brandon read a book titled No Measles, No Mumps for Me, and I asked questions, observed, and took notes. Most of Brandon's homework reading was done from books we had available at home, many of which

Brandon has heard over and over again as bedtime stories.

Brandon seldom complains about sitting to do homework. Because I returned to college when Brandon was four years old, homework became a familiar concept for him. Whenever I sat down to do homework, so did Brandon. At first it was "pretend" homework for him, coloring and drawing pictures, but then after he started kindergarten, he joined in with "real" homework, writing the alphabet and reading words.

I asked Brandon if he enjoyed reading. "No! It's boring!" he answered. I asked him if it would help to go to the library to get some "new" books. He nodded with approval, and we made plans to go the next day.

The library event was an eye-opener for me. Brandon selected historical and biographical books--stories of events and people he had heard about at school. I had never before noticed his interest in such topics. Brandon was eager to do his homework that evening. He read the first book, Louis Pasteur and his Laboratory, in fifteen minutes. I noticed he didn't look at the clock once, as he usually did, to see how much time remained for reading.

And much to my surprise, when he finished the first book he wanted to read the second book. I told him he didn't need to read anymore, but he insisted and read The Wright Brothers anyway. The second book took twenty minutes. Therefore, Brandon completed a total of thirty-five minutes of reading and he enjoyed every one of them.

Much later that evening, when the boys were getting ready for bed, I observed my husband playing his usual nighttime game with the boys. My husband, Kevin, likes to have the two boys make up stories for him. On this particular evening it was Brandon's turn. Brandon began his story, as he always did, with "Once upon a time there was a little boy." He continued, "The little boy was playing soccer, and the soccer ball got kicked out into the forest. When the little boy went to get it, a giant grizzly bear chased him."

Kevin interrupted his story. "What was the little boy's name?" Brandon answered, "Michael Jordan." "Then what happened?" asked Kevin. "A helicopter came and picked him up with a rope ladder. They took him home and he grew up to be a tall, black guy that plays basketball for the Chicago Bulls." Kevin laughed and said maybe that's why he can jump so high.

The next day I tried to get Brandon to write a story for me. He complained, saying that he hated to write. When I asked him why, he said that it takes too long.

On several occasions, at parent/teacher conferences, the teacher has pointed out to me that Brandon takes his time and writes very neatly. He is not satisfied with simply writing letters; he draws them and is careful to follow the rules he learned in kindergarten. Once, when I was trying to teach Michael to write his name, Brandon corrected me, saying that I was teaching him wrong. He told me that I was not putting tails on the back of the letters. I gave Brandon the responsibility of teaching Michael to write his name correctly. This has proven to be more productive, for Michael can now write his name correctly.

Using my experience with the reading, I decided to give more meaning to the writing task. I asked Brandon to write a letter to his grandmother. I told him he could type it on my computer if he would like. This did the trick. Brandon spent thirty minutes typing a letter to grandmother. Unfortunately, when he finished and tried to save it, he accidentally pushed the wrong command and lost his file. This was also a learning experience in word processing.

My case study of Brandon has led me to believe that more than any other technique used to encourage a child in literacy is that of putting meaning behind their learning. By letting Brandon select books he was interested in instead of just reading to practice reading, and writing a letter to grandmother instead of just writing to practice writing, he found more meaning in what otherwise could have been tedious tasks and, therefore, spent more time learning.

READING TO EDIT: TRIMMING FLABBY SENTENCES

Simple style is like white light. It is complex, but its complexity is not obvious.

—ANATOLE FRANCE

Scene: You (the writer) taking a break from editing work while you (the reader) thumb through an anthology of American literature.

"Here's something interesting," you hear yourself say. "A piece on Henry David Thoreau."

"Who?"

"Freethinker of the nineteenth century. Radical ideas about living and writing."

"Oh, yeah?"

"Yeah. Like simplify, simplify."

"Which means?"

"Get rid of the clutter. It says here how he put talk into action. On Independence Day, 1845, he moved into a little cabin he'd built just above Walden Pond, near Concord, Massachusetts. Back to the basics. No frills."

"Hmmmmm. You mean not even a VCR?"

"Same ideas about writing. Like get to the point. Be direct. Simplify."

"Okay, read a sentence."

The reader hesitates, then begins. " 'I went to the woods because I wished to live deliberately, to front only the essential facts of life, and see if I could not learn what it had to teach, and not, when I came to die, discover that I had not lived.' "

"Sort of a long sentence, isn't it?"

"Well, it's forty-four words—long by today's standards. But look closely and you'll see that every word counts. It's all bone and muscle, no flab."

"So read me another."

" 'I wanted to live deep and suck out all the marrow of life—' "

"Hey, I like that."

" '—to drive life into a corner and reduce it to its lowest terms—' "

"I see what you mean—no extra words, no flab."

"I thought you'd get the point."

"How's that?"

"Well, you're studying to be a prose surgeon. You know—'knife of the party'? A cut above the competition?"

You groan. "Back to editing," you say.

CHAPTER PREVIEW

In this chapter we'll "simplify, simplify" and front some of the essential facts of flabby writing to see what we can learn. We'll try to drive sentences into a corner and reduce them to their lowest terms. Our aim is not to write short sentences or thin, undeveloped paragraphs; it's to write lean, direct prose.

Writing simply and clearly is not easy. Anne Tyler writes that "it's hard to be simple, the hardest thing there is." On the other hand, direct writing *feels* right. "When I see a paragraph shrinking under my eyes like a strip of bacon in a skillet," Peter De Vries says, "I know I'm on the right track."

The key idea in this chapter is focus. We consider how to

give paragraphs focus in two ways—first, by narrowing topic sentences and, second, by reducing the clutter of follow-up sentences. Focusing will help you edit papers. Why? Because "the intellect is a cleaver," according to Thoreau; "it discerns and rifts its way into the secret of things."

FOCUS IN TOPIC SENTENCES

Opening sentences can either hook your readers or invite them to sleep. They point the direction for all that follows. It's tough to write smart when you open dumb.

Openers that rivet your attention have voice, set a scene, begin with action, or use dialogue or a quotation. They establish a problem, give a command, make an assertion, or map out the territory to be covered. In other words, they *do* something. Of course, in writing that explains or persuades, you can't always be dramatic with your opening sentences. Being clear is sufficient. In fact, clarity *is* dramatic, especially to readers who are used to murky prose.

As you learned in Chapters 2 and 3, the topic sentence is an opener that demands special attention. Such a sentence defines the topic that other sentences will deal with more fully. Not surprisingly, this sentence is usually more general than others that relate to it. When such a sentence serves to organize several paragraphs, not just one, it is often called a **thesis sentence.**

In what follows, we'll consider pairs of topic sentences in terms of their interest and clarity. For each pair, check what you regard as the "better" or "revised" one.

EXERCISE 5.1: COMPARING TOPIC SENTENCES

1A. My most memorable educational experience in the high school setting was something which was very unique.

1B. In high school one teacher really communicated with me.

2A. Eastern European politics demand reassessment.

2B. The whole complex question of eastern European politics is one of immensely vital importance.

3A. There is, in my most humble opinion, a proper way and an improper way to prepare oneself for an examination.

3B. When studying for an exam, one can take an intelligent approach or a suicidal one.

4A. In recent years technological change has occurred with remarkable speed.

4B. To consider just how rapidly that technological change has occurred in recent years is indeed a fascinating area.

5A. A topic sentence creates "direction" for other sentences in a paragraph.

5B. What might be defined as the "direction" for other sentences in a paragraph is created by the topic sentence.

Now compare your list of "better" or "revised" topic sentences with these: 1B, 2A, 3B, 4A, 5A.

Most people prefer 1B because it has voice and focus; its counterpart, 1A, is voiceless, even mind-numbing. Can you hear anyone *saying* sentence 1A? Probably not. In trying to sound impressive, it succeeds only in putting the reader off. The phrase *very unique* makes about as much sense as *somewhat pregnant*.

Sentence 2A is better than 2B because it is shorter, clearer, and more focused. Notice in 2B that the verb *is* joins two noun phrases, both of them abstract. This pattern, a weak verb plus long noun phrases, often signals weak writing. Incidentally, weren't you already aware that eastern European politics was "of immensely vital importance?" Sentence 2B doesn't *say* anything.

In reading 3A and 3B aloud, you hear a difference: 3A puts the writer in the spotlight; 3B focuses on the topic. In 3A, the writer is anything but "humble"; in fact, by taking center stage, the writer communicates arrogance. Sentence

3B, on the other hand, doesn't draw attention away from the topic.

Note the simplicity of sentence 4A. Most readers prefer it to 4B because it focuses on the topic—the speed of technological change—in a clear, direct way. In 4B, the writer has again taken the spotlight. How do you react when someone tries to sell you something by using words like *fascinating, important,* or *significant*? If the topic *is* fascinating, the writing will *show* it. Then the reader, not the writer, can make the judgment.

Sentences 5A and 5B differ in their style and emphasis. Sentence 5A has an active verb (*creates*), 5B a passive verb (*is created by*). Also, 5A puts emphasis on an assertion—"topic sentence creates 'direction' "—whereas 5B puts emphasis on a long noun clause serving as subject of the sentence. Although 5B is grammatically correct, most readers would prefer 5A. It has sharper focus.

NARROWING THE TOPIC FOCUS

From the examples above, you see a few things to avoid. But what should you try to *do* when revising your topic sentences? These guidelines may help with the exercise that follows.

1. Put the subject in the spotlight.

2. Speak in your own voice, not someone else's.

3. Think about what your topic sentence actually *says*.

4. Beware of exaggeration, overstatement, and pretention.

5. *Hear* where your topic sentence is "pointing" the writing.

Do these guidelines imply that you should avoid the "I" point of view or personal judgment? Not at all. Other things being equal, prose with a human voice is more likely to engage the reader. But you need to make sure that references to yourself don't deflect attention from your real subject. In other words, know what your subject is, why you are writing, and the conventions of form (including "voice") that are called for. A personal essay requires one voice, the traditional research paper another.

Shown below are sentences that can be improved by narrowing the topic focus. Reduce the clutter in these sentences by (1) taking out unnecessary words, (2) rearranging phrases, or (3) rewording for clarity. Afterward, count the words in your revised sentences, and compare your revisions with the suggested ones that follow.

EXERICSE 5.2: NARROWING TOPIC SENTENCES

PROBLEM 1. There are, in essence, two threats to the democracies of Western nations in terrorist attacks. (15 words)

REWRITE 1. _____

_____

PROBLEM 2. It now seems abundantly clear that the way we handle information will be revolutionized by microcomputers. (16 words)

REWRITE 2. _____

_____

PROBLEM 3. Perhaps one of the most interesting aspects of loneliness is the feeling of "being alone" in a crowd. (18 words)

REWRITE 3. _____

_____

PROBLEM 4. I am personally of the opinion that TV ads for children are perhaps in need of regulation by the government. (20 words)

REWRITE 4. _____

_____

PROBLEM 5. The public schools of America are faced with the monumental challenge of a restoration of excellence. (16 words)

REWRITE 5. _____

_____

PROBLEM 6. One of the most important factors in the success of a long-term relationship is a feeling of compatibility. (18 words)

REWRITE 6. _____

_____

PROBLEM 7. The terrible tragedy of the space shuttle is important due to the fact that it has had a major effect on our complacency toward the exploration of space. (28 words)

REWRITE 7. _____

_____

PROBLEM 8. There is something to be said for transferring to business colleges, which is what a substantial number of students are doing these days. (23 words)

REWRITE 8. _____

_____

PROBLEM 9. Although I don't know much about the welfare situation, it just seems to me that there has to be a better way, which is what I would like to write about here. (32 words)

REWRITE 9. _____

_____

PROBLEM 10. The essence of the argument which is to be made in this paper is that a good deal of the needless verbiage and clutter we find in modern prose tends, in a sense, to somewhat weaken the overall effect of that writing. (42 words)

REWRITE 10. _____

_____

Here are some revisions to compare with yours: (sentence 1) Terrorist attacks present two threats to Western democracies (8 words); (sentence 2) Clearly, microcomputers will revolutionize how we handle information (8 words); (sentence 3) A person can feel alone, or "lonely," in a crowd (10 words); (sentence 4) In my opinion, TV ads for children need government regulation (10 words); (sentence 5) American public schools face the challenge of restoring excellence (9 words); (sentence 6) Successful marriages result when people genuinely like each other (9 words); (sentence 7) The space-shuttle tragedy ended our complacency toward space exploration (10 words); (sentence 8) Many students today seem to be transferring to business colleges (10 words); (sentence 9) Certain critical problems in the welfare system need addressing (9 words); (sentence 10) My argument is that needless clutter weakens modern prose (9 words).

By whispering each sentence and then its revision—and weighing the effect of each—you will begin to sense what Thoreau was saying: *Simplify, simplify.*

WRITING TO THE POINT

Let's now shift our attention from topic sentences to sentences in general. The emphasis here is on **writing to the point**—in other words, reducing needless clutter in prose.

When you cut through padding, your writing becomes less redundant.

For example, in each of these pairs of words, one will do.

each and every	first and foremost
any and all	hopes and desires
hope and trust	basic and fundamental
full and complete	totally and completely

You can slice through the redundant categories (color, size, type, kind, and so on) in phrases such as these:

red in color	huge in size
a period of time	few in number
a square shape	various differences
today's modern world	final concluding summary
a crisis-type situation	aggressive kind of behavior

Redundant modifiers—for example, *"personal* opinion"—offer further opportunities to cut through flab. (Of course your opinion is personal; would you offer an impersonal opinion?) Study the redundant modifiers below, and sharpen your scalpel:

past history	future plans
end result	mix together
unintended accident	discarded litter
final outcome	terrible tragedy
basic essentials	close proximity
repeat again	circle around
refer back	continue on

Now examine the following list of commonly used flabby phrases, noting how a one-word option can do the work of several words:

Flabby Phrases	One-Word Options
due to the fact that	because
the reason for this is	since
for the reason that	as, since, because
in view of the fact that	because

on the occasion of	when
in the event of	if, when
the way in which	how
despite the fact that	although
regardless of the fact that	although
the question of whether or not	whether
come to the realization that	realize
of the opinion that	think
aware of the fact that	know
make an adjustment in	adjust
come in contact with	meet
there is a need for	must
it is necessary that	must
there is a possibility that	may, might, could
it could happen that	may, might, could
has the ability to	can
for the purpose of	for, to
in close proximity to	near
concerning the matter of	about, concerning
prior to	before
subsequent to	after
at this point in time	now
at that point in time	then
with regard (reference) to	about
to the effect that	that
as a matter of fact	actually

Finally, it perhaps goes without saying that you can improve your sentences by cutting a rather broad range of qualifiers—such as *perhaps, goes without saying,* and *rather*—not to mention words and phrases such as *really, apparently, seems, somewhat, possibly, tends, to a certain extent,* and *not to mention.*

You can practice trimming flab from sentences in the exercise that follows. Read each sentence carefully; then cut through the flab on the lines below. Afterward, compare your rewritten sentences with the suggested answers.

EXERCISE 5.3: TRIMMING SENTENCE FLAB

PROBLEM 1. Due to the fact that I must work my way through college, I have come to the realization that education is rather expensive. (23 words)

REWRITE 1. _____

_____

PROBLEM 2. I am also aware of the fact that I must make an adjustment, to some extent, in my hopes and desires to graduate in four years. (26 words)

REWRITE 2. _____

_____

PROBLEM 3. Prior to my realization-type experience, I perhaps had a considerable number of somewhat unrealistic expectations concerning the matter of college expenses. (21 words)

REWRITE 3. _____

_____

PROBLEM 4. Regardless of the fact that I had talked with a college counselor, it was nevertheless my personal opinion that my future plans for a certain kind of sports car were not incompatible with college. (34 words)

REWRITE 4. _____

_____

PROBLEM 5. Be that as it may, at this point in time I have had to take out a loan for the purpose of continuing on with my course work. (27 words)

REWRITE 5. _____

_____

Compare your revised sentences with these: (sentence 1) Because I must work my way through college, I realize that education is expensive (14 words); (sentence 2) I also realize that I must adjust my hope to graduate in four years (14 words); (sentence 3) Before my realization, I had many unrealistic expectations about college expenses (11 words); (sentence 4) Although I had talked with a counselor, I still believed that my plans for a sports car were compatible with college (21 words); (sentence 5) However, I now have had to take out a loan to continue my course work (15 words).

MORE ON SENTENCE SURGERY

To provide focus for the practice that follows, Exercise 5.4 presents seven suggestions for sentence surgery. Each suggestion is first presented in the form of short "kernel" (or sentence-combining) sentences.

Study each sentence-combining exercise; then read the accompanying problem sentence. Use the lines below to rewrite the sentence in a clear, direct way. Count the words of each rewritten sentence.

EXERCISE 5.4: SEVEN SUGGESTIONS FOR SENTENCE SURGERY

1. Use active verbs.
   Avoid the passive voice.
   Avoid it whenever possible.

PROBLEM 1. Verbs that are characterized by activity are to be used, and the passive type of voice is, whenever it is at all possible, to be avoided. (26 words)

REWRITE 1. _____

_____

2. Choose wording.
   The wording is straightforward.
   Don't choose diction.
   The diction is pretentious.
   The diction is trendy.

PROBLEM 2. Wording which has the extraordinarily important quality of straightforwardness is to be chosen over diction which is self-conscious or even, for that matter, unconsciously pretentious per se; by the same token, with-it (or, shall we say, trendy) diction just doesn't cut it, writingwise. (43 words)

REWRITE 2. _____

_____

3. Trim adjectives.
   Trim adverbs.
   Trim vague ones in particular.
   Trim obvious ones in particular.
   Trim redundant ones in particular.

PROBLEM 3. It is extremely, indeed vitally, important to trim extra and excessive adjectival and adverbial modifiers, most particularly the vague, general, empty ones; the obvious, needless, and unessential ones; and last, but most assuredly not least, the inanely repetitious and/or redundant ones. (41 words)

REWRITE 3. _____

_____

4. Reduce clauses to phrases.
   The clauses are cumbersome.

Reduce phrases to modifiers.
The phrases are lengthy.
The modifiers have one word.

PROBLEM 4. There are any number of clauses that are cumbersome which can go through a process of reduction to become phrases, and there are also many lengthy phrases in the sentence with a function of modification that can be reduced to single words. (42 words)

REWRITE 4. _____

_____

5. Rework sentences.
   The sentences are bloated with nouns.
   The nouns are abstract.
   Shorten noun phrases.
   Shorten them whenever possible.

PROBLEM 5. It is suggested that the bloating of the structure of nominalization is cause for the reworking of the noun phrase component of the sentential unit in the direction of abbreviating said structure so as to reduce its level of abstraction. (40 words)

REWRITE 5. _____

_____

6. Eliminate qualifiers.
   The qualifiers are unneeded.
   Eliminate any pileup of phrases.
   The phrases are prepositional.

PROBLEM 6. To be sure, any unneeded qualifier is more or less unnecessary and should probably therefore be eliminated, as is also perhaps the case, in a sense, with the pileup of phrases of various prepositions in the context of the sentence. (40 words)

REWRITE 6. _____

_____

7. Make shifts in direction clear.
   Use signal words.
   The signal words are explicit.

PROBLEM 7. The shifting of directionality should, by all means, be clear though the utilization of words that sort of "signal," so to speak, in an explicit manner rather than implicit manner. (30 words)

REWRITE 7. _____

_____

Now compare your seven rewrites with the ones that follow. (The problem sentences contain a total of 262 words; the revised sentences below contain a total of 74 words.)

1. Use active verbs, avoiding the passive voice whenever possible. (9 words)

2. Choose straightforward wording rather than pretentious or trendy diction. (9 words)

3. Trim adjectives and adverbs, particularly vague, obvious, and redundant ones. (10 words)

4. Reduce cumbersome clauses to phrases, and reduce lengthy phrases to one-word modifiers. (13 words)

5. Rework sentences that are bloated with abstract nouns, and shorten noun phrases whenever possible. (14 words)

6. Eliminate unneeded qualifiers and any pileup of prepositional phrases. (9 words)

7. Use explicit signal words to make shifts in direction clear. (10 words)

You may wonder about some of the terms used in the preceding exercise. The key to understanding these terms is knowing that each problem sentence breaks the rule it supposedly expresses. The revised sentences, on the other hand, *illustrate* the principles being discussed. Thus if you want to know what *passive voice* means, examine problem 1. Its counterpart, rewrite 1, illustrates active voice.

By studying the problem sentences and each rewrite, you'll quickly learn several key concepts for revising your own writing. We'll apply these concepts in Exercise 5.5.

APPLYING THE SEVEN SUGGESTIONS

Use the seven suggestions for sentence surgery in the following exercise. Reduce the clutter in the problem sentences by combining the short sentences in a clear, direct way. Put your revision on the rewrite lines. After doing the exercise, count the words in each revision and compare. By reading the problem and rewrite sentences side by side, you'll see and hear the differences.

EXERCISE 5.5: THOREAU'S PROSE
(Trimming Flab)

1. Thoreau's writing deals with themes.
   The themes are philosophical.
   His approach is straightforward.
   His approach is not abstract

PROBLEM 1. Philosophical themes are dealt with in the writing of Thoreau, but the approach is a straightforward one rather than one given to abstraction. (23 words)

REWRITE 1. _____

2. He refuses to compromise his style.
   Compromise would be with qualifiers.
   Compromise would be with extra modifiers.
   Compromise would be with overstatement.

PROBLEM 2. There is a refusal by Thoreau to compromise
the effectiveness of his style with language that qualifies, adds
extra modifiers, or in any way overstates matters. (26 words)

REWRITE 2. _____

_____

3. His voice is clear.
   He favors sentences with verbs.
   The verbs are active.
   He favors sentences with subjects.
   The subjects are concrete.

PROBLEM 3. It is because of his predilection for sentences
characterized by active verbs and concrete subjects that his
voice is clear. (20 words)

REWRITE 3. _____

_____

4. He engages the reader.
   He addresses questions.
   The questions are profound.
   They deal with human meanings.
   They deal with human values.
   He uses a down-to-earth manner.

PROBLEM 4. His engagement with the reader is a result of
the fact that there are profound questions of human meanings
and values which are addressed in a down-to-earth sort of
manner. (30 words)

REWRITE 4. _____

_____

5. He uses language. (in other words)
   He uncovers his subject matter.
   He doesn't use language to obscure it.

PROBLEM 5. In other words, instead of using language in an obfuscatory way, language is used by Thoreau to uncover his subject matter. (21 words)

REWRITE 5. _____

_____

   Now compare your revisions with the ones that follow. (The problem sentences contain a total of 120 words; the revised sentences contain a total of 69 words.)

1. Thoreau's writing deals with philosophical themes, but his approach is straightforward, not abstract. (13 words)

2. He refuses to compromise his style with qualifiers, extra modifiers, or overstatement. (12 words)

3. His voice is clear because he favors active verbs and concrete subjects. (12 words)

4. He engages the reader by addressing profound questions of human meanings and values in a down-to-earth manner. (17 words)

5. In other words, he uses language to uncover his subject matter, not to obscure it. (15 words)

   Let's now consider the weaknesses in the problem sentences. In problem 1, you see passive voice and abstract-noun phrases. In problem 2, you see a "deadwood" opener, passive voice, bloated-noun phrases, and unnecessary modifiers. In problem 3, you again see a "deadwood" opener, plus the other problems mentioned above. In problem 4, you see a pileup of phrases and clauses in addition to passive voice. In problem 5, you see yet another instance of passive construction and extra modifiers.
   In short, all of the problem sentences illustrate grammati-

cally correct—but dreadful—writing. The rewrite sentences, on the other hand, are clear and easy to read.

LOOKING BACK, LOOKING AHEAD

As we've seen in this chapter, simplifying your prose does not mean being simpleminded. Nor does it mean writing "Dick-and-Jane" style sentences with little variety. Writing lean, direct prose is hard work; and many people obscure the obvious to cover up the fact that they have little to say.

Regrettably, many schools and government agencies encourage a puffed-up, self-important style. Don't be misled. Stringing together a series of abstractions or overly ornate descriptions serves only to put readers off. However much this sort of writing may try to impress, it often has the unmistakable smell of sewer sludge. Know that if you write it intentionally—you can no longer do so out of ignorance—you will surely clog your own pipes.

You were given seven suggestions for sentence surgery in this chapter. Review those suggestions before you tackle the exercises that follow. Perhaps the most basic suggestion of all is to reread aloud whatever you write, asking yourself, What does this mean? In doing so, you'll see that Thoreau was on the right track: *Simplify, simplify.* In Chapter 6, we'll examine what you can do to proofread your own prose.

 ## DO-IT-YOURSELF EXERCISES

Please be prepared to share your work in class. Your instructor will provide suggested answers for Exercises 5.6–5.9. Use Exercise 5.10 to make a personal application of trimming flab from sentences.

EXERCISE 5.6: FOCUS IN TOPIC SENTENCES

Directions: Sharpen the focus for the following topic sentences by cutting through flab and padding. Count the words in your revised sentences, and compare your revisions with the problem sentences.

PROBLEM 1. At the present point in time, it now seems clear that two-thirds of all American mothers are in the labor force outside the home, which is to say approximately double the rate of 1955. (34 words)

REWRITE 1. _____

_____

PROBLEM 2. As a result of the fact that the rate of divorce has doubled since 1965, it is now predicted by sociologists who study such matters that half of today's contemporary marriages will ultimately end in divorce. (36 words)

REWRITE 2. _____

_____

PROBLEM 3. As I have learned from many countless hours in the library doing the research for this paper, the whole definition of just what makes up what we call a *family* has, to a very great extent, changed in recent years. (40 words)

REWRITE 3. _____

_____

PROBLEM 4. In the early years of the 1970s, perhaps the most cherished value that was held by many of the freshman students at the college level was "developing a meaningful philosophy of life," but it seems that this value had dropped to ninth by 1990. (44 words)

REWRITE 4. _____

_____

PROBLEM 5. Thanks to the political policies of the 1980s, there are now reliable government statistics to show that the richest 20 percent of American citizens receive 44 percent of the national family income, whereas the poorest 20 percent of American citizens get ony 4.6 percent of the national family income. (49 words)

REWRITE 5. _____

_____

EXERCISE 5.7: FRIDAY-NIGHT CONCERT
(Trimming Flab)

Directions: Each set of kernel (or sentence-combining) sentences is followed by a problem sentence. Use the lines below to rewrite sentences in a clear, direct way. Count the words in the rewrite sentences, and compare these sentences with the problem sentences.

1. The auditorium was like a steam bath.
   It was sweltering.
   It was jammed with thousands of students.
   They had finished their midterm exams.
   They now wanted some Friday-night excitement.

PROBLEM 1. There was an auditorium that was sweltering like a steam bath, and it was exceedingly jammed with thousands of students, each of whom had finished his or her midterm exams and now wanted some excitement on this particular Friday night. (40 words)

REWRITE 1. _____

_____

2. The students had waited for nearly an hour.
   They had sipped soft drinks.
   They had eaten popcorn.
   Now their patience was wearing thin.

PROBLEM 2. It was after a wait of nearly an hour, during which time the students had sipped a variety of soft drinks and eaten popcorn sold by vendors, that their patience was now wearing somewhat thin, to say the least. (39 words)

REWRITE 2. ——————————————————————————

——

3. A chant erupted.
   It was rhythmic.
   It spread up the rows.
   It brought the crowd to its feet.
   It demanded music.

PROBLEM 3. Eventually erupting from the crowd was a chant, the rhythms of which spread up the rows toward the top of the auditorium and brought the audience to its feet, where it stood and demanded music. (35 words)

REWRITE 3. ——————————————————————————

——

4. Colored lights swirled through the crowd.
   The chant grew in intensity.
   It swelled like a bubble.
   The swelling was dangerous.
   The bubble might burst.

PROBLEM 4. As a really fabulous array of colored lights swirled this way and that through the crowd in the auditorium, the chant grew in intensity, swelling larger and larger like a bubble in possible danger of being about to burst. (39 words)

REWRITE 4. ——————————————————————————

——

5. Then the stage exploded with light.
   The stage had been darkened.
   The explosion was sudden.
   The light was brilliant.
   The stage exploded with sound.
   The sound pounded the senses.

PROBLEM 5. It was not too long thereafter that the stage, which had been previously darkened, all of a sudden seemed to explode with light as well as with sound, and it was this sound that pounded the senses of the crowd. (40 words)

REWRITE 5. _____

_____

6. The crowd went wild.
   It screamed with one voice.
   The voice was joyful.
   The voice was delirious.

PROBLEM 6. The crowd went absolutely and completely wild with incredibly awesome excitement, and its scream seemed to be with one voice that was both resonant with joy and, to put it mildly, somewhat delirious. (33 words)

REWRITE 6. _____

_____

EXERCISE 5.8: WRITER AS READER
(Trimming Flab)

Directions: Each set of kernel (or sentence-combining) sentences is followed by a problem sentence. Use the lines below to rewrite sentences in a clear, direct way. Count the words in the rewrite sentences, and compare these sentences with the problem sentences.

1. The human brain processes the world.
   It tries to make sense of everything.
   This includes words in print.

PROBLEM 1. The brain of the human being is engaged in
the processing of the world and makes an effort to come to
an understanding of everything, including words in the context
of print. (32 words)

REWRITE 1. _____

_____

2. It searches for meaning.
   It connects words.
   It connects sentences.
   It connects paragraphs.

PROBLEM 2. As a result of its search for meaningful
interpretations, individual words, sentential units, and
paragraph structures are connected. (18 words)

REWRITE 2. _____

_____

3. This fact suggests something.
   Writing is a one-way conversation.
   The conversation is with an audience.
   The audience is invisible.

PROBLEM 3. What is suggested by this fact is that the nature
of writing is a one-way conversation with an audience that
remains invisible. (22 words)

REWRITE 3. _____

_____

4. The audience cannot ask questions.
   The writer must anticipate the reader's needs.
   The writer must question the text.
   The writer must try to provide answers.

PROBLEM 4. Because of the inability of the audience to ask questions, the needs of the reader must be anticipated by the writer, who must then engage in a questioning of the text in an effort to provide answers. (37 words)

REWRITE 4. _____

_____

5. This process involves imagination.
   The writer must "become" the intended reader.
   The reader sees the text for the first time.
   The reader perhaps dislikes its dull opening.
   The reader perhaps misunderstands its key terms.

PROBLEM 5. Involvement of the imaginative aspect is fundamental to this process because the person engaged in the activity of writing must "become," in some sense, the intended reader, who, in an initial encounter of perceiving the text, may perhaps have feelings of antipathy for its dull opening and/or not be fully cognizant of its essential nomenclature (i.e., terminology). (56 words)

REWRITE 5. _____

_____

6. Such reading may be very difficult.
   It underlies revision.
   Revision is the act of "seeing again."
   "Seeing again" often leads to clarity.

PROBLEM 6. While it is true that there may be extraordinary difficulty in this sort of reading, it is also true that reading of this kind is what underlies revision itself, the act of "seeing again" that more often than not leads to some measure of clarity (or, more precisely, reduced obfuscation). (50 words)

REWRITE 6. _____

_____

EXERCISE 5.9: PYRAMID SCHEMES
(Trimming Flab)

Directions: Each set of kernel (or sentence-combining) sentences is followed by a problem sentence. Use the lines below to rewrite sentences in a clear, direct way. Count the words in the rewrite sentences, and compare these sentences with the problem sentences.

1. Chain letters are pyramid schemes.
   The schemes promise great rewards.
   The rewards are for an investment.
   The investment is a one-time one.

PROBLEM 1. The chain letter is one type of scheme known as the *pyramid,* which has the promise of great rewards if a person is willing to make an investment just one time. (31 words)

REWRITE 1. _____

_____

2. No product is being sold.
   No service is being sold.
   Profits result from recruiting others.
   Recruitment is into the scheme.

PROBLEM 2. In spite of the fact that it is entirely obvious that no product is being sold—nor, for that matter, any service either—profits result from the recruitment of others into the scheme. (33 words)

REWRITE 2. _____

_____

3. Each new member pays a sum.
   The sum goes to others in the chain.
   Each new member tries to recruit outsiders.
   Recruitment is to keep the pyramid building.

PROBLEM 3. After having made the payment of a sum to other individuals in the chain, each new member makes an effort in the recruitment of outsiders in order to sustain the upward momentum of the pyramid's growth. (36 words)

REWRITE 3. _____

_____

4. Something is unfortunate.
   Mathematical probability has its laws.
   Only 10 percent of investors are rewarded.
   Over 50 percent lose their investment.

PROBLEM 4. Although it is rather unfortunate for investors, mathematical probability does indeed have its laws, and as a consequence of this fact, only 10 percent of the individuals who make an investment receive any kind of reward, whereas over 50 percent of investors lose what they have put into it. (49 words)

REWRITE 4. _____

_____

5. This fact escapes many people.
   The fact is simple.
   They are duped by promotions.
   They are duped by business ventures.
   These are built on pyramid schemes.

PROBLEM 5. This fact, however plain and simple it may be, somehow seems to escape many of the persons who are, to some extent, duped by the various kinds of promotions and assorted business ventures that have been built upon the scheme which, for purposes of our discussion, we have called the *pyramid*. (50 words)

REWRITE 5. _____

_____

6. Among these ventures are distributorships.
   The distributorships are multilevel.
   An investor purchases products.
   The products can be sold at a profit.
   The profit is modest.

PROBLEM 6. Among these various and assorted ventures are what might be called *multilevel distributorships,* the idea of which is for the individual investor to make the purchase of products so that he or she can, in turn, sell these products at a profit, albeit a modest one. (46 words)

REWRITE 6. ——————————————————————

——————————————————————

7. The big money comes from recruiting others.
   One earns commissions on their sales.

PROBLEM 7. It is from the recuitment of others that substantial sums of remuneration are achieved, owing to the fact that commissions are earned on the sales of these recruited individuals. (29 words)

REWRITE 7. ——————————————————————

——————————————————————

8. Many investors are unaware of something.
   The real product is not cosmetics.
   The real product is not vitamins.
   The real product is not soap.
   The real product is the distributorship itself.

PROBLEM 8. Although it may not be immediately apparent to the unaware type of investor, the real product that is being sold is not cosmetics, not vitamins, and not soap, but another product altogether—the distributorship itself. (35 words)

REWRITE 8. ——————————————————————

——————————————————————

9. All pyramid schemes collapse.
   The collapse is inevitable.
   The supply of new recruits runs out.
   The new recruits are earnest.
   The promoters move on.
   The promoters pocket their profits.

PROBLEM 9. The inevitable collapse of all pyramid schemes comes when the supply of these earnest persons who have been newly recruited eventually runs out, and those behind the promotion move on to other areas, with profits in their pockets. (38 words)

REWRITE 9. _____

_____

EXERCISE 5.10: PERSONAL APPLICATION

In this chapter you've learned a variety of ways to trim flab from sentences. The seven suggestions for stronger sentences will be helpful as you work to make your own writing lean, direct, and to the point.

Find at least three paragraphs of some work in progress that you'd like to improve stylistically. The content and organization of this writing should already be established. Make photocopies of the paragraphs.

Now count the words in each sentence of your paragraphs, and write these word counts after each sentence. On a separate sheet of paper, rewrite the sentences in the flabbiest style you can manage. In other words, work hard to *break* all of the rules for lean, direct writing. Concentrate on making your prose as dreadful as possible without making any real changes in its content or organization. Count the words in each sentence of your flabby writing; once again, write the word counts after each sentence.

Return now to your original version. On another sheet of paper, use the seven suggestions for stronger sentences to rewrite your prose in as lean and direct a fashion as possible, again without changing its content or organization. Make this writing the best you can manage. Then count the words in each sentence; write the word count after each sentence.

You should now have three versions of your paper, ranging from "flabby" to "lean and direct." Create a chart like this one to compare the number of words in the sentences in your three writing samples.

SENTENCE COMPARISON (WORD COUNT)

	Flabby Version	Original Version	Lean Version
1.	32	23	16
2.	40	30	15
3.	35	25	17

and so on

Now take your flabby version and swap with someone else in class. As this person attempts to make your deliberately dreadful writing lean and direct, you should be doing the same with his or hers. After doing your best, check the numbers on your partner's sentence-comparison chart. How close did you come to his or her lean version?

This process of deliberately altering the style of your writing may well have resulted in some personal insights. What did you learn from the process? Write up what you learned in the form of a paragraph. Make reference to your sentence-comparison chart as appropriate.

Hand in your work from this application activity. Your packet of materials should contain the following: (1) photocopies of four original paragraphs; (2) the two revised versions of your original work, one flabby, the other lean and direct; (3) your sentence comparison of the three versions; and (4) one or more paragraphs describing what you learned from this activity.

PROSE SURGERY IN ACTION

"My idea of writing used to be 'the more the better,'" writes Duane Peck, who used to try to impress his instructors with big words and writing that sounded "academic." Now, however, he believes that "simplicity is the key to effective writing."

Over a ten-week period, Duane worked to correct his overwriting problem. While the positive changes were noticeable to everyone, Duane was especially pleased: "[As the term progressed] my sentence structure was not only more readable and easy to understand, but also contained variety. My papers were more interesting to read. But, most important of all, they began to sound like me."

For Duane, learning to write simply and directly was not easy. On a problem/solution assignment, for example, his response draft was bloated and ponderous, difficult to read. While his conference draft showed some progress, the strategy of using a dictionary definition did little to "hook" the reader's interest. On his final draft, however, Duane cut through the vagueness, abstraction, and passive voice to get specific and engage the reader. "Rereading several times," he says, led to these improvements and helped uncover his personal voice.

Here are the four symbols used in class and in conferences to prompt revision and editing:

+ = I like this [word, phrase, sentence].

√ = Please check this [word, phrase, sentence].

? = I don't follow this [word, phrase, sentence).

= Think about developing this part more.

Are Educators Professionals?
(Response Draft)

wordiness [There are many issues concerning the world of education today. Many issues are interwoven within each other making it difficult to distinguish the effect each separate issue has on education as a whole.] Although there may be other explanations to many educational problems being considered, I will explore the question, "Are educators professionals?"

Before I attempt to define what a professional is, I feel it is necessary to consider why such a question should be asked. First, it seems to me that much of a person's abilities *ability* to be a productive, functioning member of society rely *relies* on the perception a person may have of himself or herself. Some of this perception comes from the importance society places on the person and the occupation the person may be in. For example, good doctors and lawyers are perceived as being essential to *wordiness* *example* the way we live today. On the other hand, in some ways many people treat teachers as something expendable. Some of these ways include salaries, community support, recognition, and (lack of) appropriate respect. When a person is treated as *as* less than he or she deserves it has an effect on that persons *'s* performance.

[*The above draft goes on to reassert that "many of the issues in education could be effectively dealt with if the importance of the teaching profession were recognized."*]

Are Educators Professionals?
(Conference Draft)

Webster's New Collegiate Dictionary defines professional as
1. Of or pertaining to a profession; as, professional standards,
and 2. Characteristic of or conforming to the standards of a
profession. What then does it mean to be a professional?

From this definition one must be engaged in a profession,
and work to uphold the ethics and standards that make that
profession unique and valuable. Meeting these standards in
education requires self-discipline and training. Not only must
a person meet high standards in his or her area of emphasis,
but also complete an extensive study in the field of education.
For many, myself included, this amount of training takes from
five to six years to complete. Many find it desirable, if not
necessary to go beyond these basic requirements and achieve
a Masters or a Doctorate level. This alone should qualify a
person for the title of a professional.

However, there is more. If the education system is working
properly teachers are evaluated on a regular basis to see if
they are meeting the standards and ethics of education. If they
are not then steps are taken to help the teacher meet acceptable
standards of performance. As with any other profession, if
standards are not met, and the teacher does not improve, they
must be forced to find another occupation in which they can
meet the standards required.

[*This draft goes on to compare the recognition given to teachers
with that given to professional athletes and argues for redefin-
ing our society's priorities.*]

Are Educators Professionals?
by
Duane Peck

Although many issues regarding the field of education exist today, few are as significant as the question, Are teachers professionals?

Much of a person's ability to be a productive, functioning member of society depends on a person's self-perception. Some of this perception comes from the importance society places on the person and the occupation the person may be in. For example, good doctors and lawyers are perceived as being essential to the way we live today. On the other hand, teachers receive little by way of salaries, community support, recognition, and appropriate respect.

In today's society, the influence of a job is often reflected by the salary received by employees. Examples of prestigious occupations include doctors, lawyers, professional athletes, and some top corporate positions. Teachers are no less valuable to society than these positions, yet some teacher salaries are comparable to that of the local garbage collector. This message implies that teachers are not important and that they have no influence on our future as a society.

In addition, when a particular occupation is seen as trivial, people will not support the employees of that occupation. For example, while attending high school, I participated in the drama program. The stage we had to work with was substandard in almost every respect, especially in the electrical wiring. Many times the fuse panel would actually spark during performances. Yet with all of these problems, our teacher could not raise enough support to have the wiring upgraded to a safe operating level. This type of situation reflects the casual attitudes many have towards the educational process.

Recognition is another aspect of professionalism that makes a difference in forming public opinion. Big-name professional athletes are a good example. When the name Michael Jordan is mentioned, almost everyone who has come in contact with basketball knows who he is and what he has accomplished. But not many teachers today are known outside their immediate areas.

All of these attitudes determine to a large degree the respect people have for an occupation. What kind of respect are we passing on to future generations when some teachers must teach in a bulletproof cage? Partly because of the lack of respect given to teachers, many bright and talented young people are looking into other occupations rather than becoming teachers. This loss is inestimable and also unnecessary.

There is one other person to consider when dealing with teaching, the student. Although many teachers do their best to provide a more than adequate education under less than favorable circumstances, it is the student who suffers in the end. Because we are selling our teachers short, we are selling the future of our children short. In the end, the students are the ones who must suffer the consequences of our actions.

From this perspective, the future may look dismal, but it doesn't need to remain that way. Although it will take time, we can change the attitudes of people towards education. The first step is to make the public aware that teachers are professionals in their own right and deserve to be treated as such. Parents of students need to become aware of the training required to become public educators, as well as the challenges teachers face in the educational process. Seminars and other public meetings, headed by an authority in the field of education, could be held to acquaint parents with many educational problems being faced today.

Students also need to become actively aware of the issues that affect them and their future. To accomplish this task, schools could bring in special speakers to educate students on such educational issues. Following such an event, students should be given the opportunity to provide possible solutions. This would allow students to become involved and would help them understand what they can do to further the education process.

The most important element of the solution is recognition. Most teachers today are not teaching for money or personal gratification. Their purpose is to prepare students for the future. Such people deserve to be recognized for their contributions and dedication to society. If teachers were to receive the recognition they deserve, more talented individuals would consider teaching as a possible career choice, and teacher morale, as well as the quality of education, would increase. Recognition is a small price to pay for such large returns.

Once parents and students understand the importance of education, support for teachers will increase, government officials will be more willing to attempt to solve the financial problems facing education, and teachers will be able to focus on preparing their students for the future.

When education achieves its rightful place among the "learned professions," we will be able to deal with other issues more effectively. Some issues may even vanish because education will require more of those teaching, as well as those who are learning. After all, if we didn't have any teachers, who would prepare the future doctors, lawyers, and even athletes that are so indispensible to us today?

6

Editor

READING TO EDIT: CORRECTING SENTENCE ERRORS

I can't write five words but that I change seven.
—DOROTHY PARKER

Scene: You and members of your response group huddled over photocopies of your paper as you get ready to read aloud

"Okay, how do we do this?" somebody asks. "I don't know what we're doing."

"I'll read slowly," you say. "You make notes in the margin—or on the page—to give me feedback."

"What kind of notes?"

You grin at the others. "If you didn't cut class all the time, you'd understand this stuff about editing."

"I'm studying sleep disorders. You know, in the library? Of course, I can sleep anywhere—"

You pull a class handout from your notebook. "Look, here are the symbols we're supposed to use. It's a kind of shorthand for making notes on our drafts."

Giving Feedback

Make marginal notes, using these four symbols.

Then give constructive feedback to the writer.

+ = I like this [word, phrase, sentence].

√ = Please check this [word, phrase, sentence].

? = I don't follow this [word, phrase, sentence].

= Think about developing this part more.

Others in the group have already begun to read your paper silently, their pencils poised.

"Yeah, but what's the point?"

"The point? Letting me know what works and what doesn't. You make notes so you can remember what you want to bring to my attention."

"I don't understand the check mark."

"That's for any errors you spot. You know, like misspelled words, punctuation problems, whatever. Anything that doesn't sound right or look right."

"I'm not much good at proofreading."

"Some of us aren't either. But four heads are better than one. The whole idea is to work together—to learn from each other."

"What if I'm not sure about something?"

"Just check it. Afterward, it's my job to find out whether there's really a problem."

"So how do you do that?"

"Dictionary. Thesaurus. Grammar handbook."

A member of your response group looks up. "Ready to get started?"

"Sure," you nod. "Let's go."

CHAPTER PREVIEW

Chapters 4 and 5 emphasized close reading to check for coherence and to trim flab from sentences. This chapter builds on the concept of close reading, focusing on the basics of editing and proofreading. We consider what you can do to improve sentence-level mechanics through proofreading.

Like Chapter 5, this chapter uses sentence-combining exercises, this time to focus on basic skills—sentence structure, usage, and conventions of spelling, punctuation, and capitalization. Working through the material that follows will prepare you for the practice exercises. The exercises, in turn, will help build skills that you can apply to your writing in progress.

It's appropriate for us to deal with "correctness" late in the writing process. The early stages of revising focused on the larger issues of content and organization (What are the main points I want to make? How can I organize to accomplish my aims?). At this stage of editing, these issues should be resolved. The question now is, How can I write effectively and correctly?

PROOFREADING IN PERSPECTIVE

Let's suppose you're reading a sentence and you come across a misspelled wird—as you just did. What is your reaction? Do you "read through" the misspelling, concentrating on the meaning of the sentence, or do you momentarily lose your concentration?

For most readers, errors in spelling, punctuation, and usage interrupt their reading. Each error, like a pothole in the road, deflects the reader's attention from the surrounding view. If the road is rough enough, the potholes *consume* one's attention.

In other words, deviations from standard English are not "bad" in some moral sense. They are, instead, sources of needless irritation. So while *wird* may "communicate," it does so only if the reader makes a special effort to decode the nonstandard spelling. Most readers, yourself included, have better things to do than try to outguess a careless writer.

It makes no difference how interesting, profound, or well-reasoned the message is. An irritated reader eventually stops reading. Because of this fact of human nature, writer William

Zinsser advises that you must "take an obsessive pride in the smallest details of your craft." To edit carefully means to "sweat the details."

Perhaps you've never thought of writing or reading as a game, but it is, in many ways. Right now, for example, you expect certain things of the text you are reading. At a minimum, you expect it to be truthful, well organized, and free from surface errors. While these expectations aren't necessarily conscious, they're still very real. If you encountered errors here, you would make a judgment about the value of the entire message. "If the writer doesn't care enough to edit and proofread," you would say to yourself, "why should I take the message seriously?"

In early stages of revising, as noted above, you try to get your content and organization clear. You ask, What am I really trying to say? How can I reorganize this text? As you concentrate on editing and proofreading, however, your questions shift to What can I do to tighten my language? Do quotation marks go inside or outside the commas? Which word seems to work better here? Such questions help you put your writing in final form.

A PROOFREADING PRETEST

Before getting to exercises that will tune up your proofreading skills, let's find out what you are already able to do. The proofreading pretest focuses on a number of subskills in proofreading.

In each of the first thirty sentences below, you'll find a single error. Put a check mark above each one. Since the last ten sentences contain two errors each, put two check marks at the appropriate places. Then consult the answer key that follows.

There are a total of fifty items in the pretest. Each item is worth two points. See how many points you can get *before* turning to the answer key.

EXERCISE 6.1: A PROOFREADING PRETEST
(100 Points)

1. See if you can spot the mispelling here.

2. Errors in Capitalization, as shown here, sometimes result from trying to emphasize a word.

3. This sentence, which may prove tricky has an error in punctuation between the subject and verb.

4. If your skillful, you will identify a single spelling error here.

5. Here you may find a sentence fragment. Especially if you look closely.

6. A writer may put in extra words, as you can see here, in in the process of writing.

7. On the other hand, a writer sometimes leaves words when writing quickly.

8. Dropping word endings, as in this sentence, can also interrupt a reader comprehension.

9. Dropping verb endings create special problems in subject/verb agreement.

10. If you switch verb tenses, as in this sentence, you confused your readers.

11. The comma splice, as shown here, is a very common error, it should be rewritten or punctuated correctly.

12. Related to the comma splice is the run-on sentence it tries to fuse two closely related sentences.

13. Although you may overlook the missing comma after an introductory clause you should look more closely.

14. Commas normally separate the clauses in compound sentences but some writers forget to put them in.

15. You may put in unnecessary commas, because you don't read sentences carefully, listening for pauses.

16. A nicely structured sentence can be ruined while a writer uses the wrong conjunction.

17. A person which is not proofreading may make errors with relative pronouns (*who, whom, which, that, whose*).

18. Some sentences are rather difficult to read that put modifying clauses in the wrong place.

19. Trying to make more mature sentences, dangling modifiers are sometimes created by writers.

20. It is easy to forget that each pronoun should agree with their antecedent.

21. Alot of readers get upset when writers blend two simple words together—as shown here.

22. An other kind of spelling error, which is illustrated, results from splitting one word in two.

23. It's unfortunate when you don't catch simple errors with apostrophe's in your proofreading.

24. To unthinkingly and repeatedly split infinitives is a common, but often unnoticed, error.

25. Although you may take idioms for granite, they also can present problems.

26. Looking at prepositions, you quickly arrive to the conclusion that they can make a real difference.

27. To write well, a writer should not shift your point of view.

28. Slang-type stuff, as in this sentence, should certainly be edited.

29. Some expressions, however totally awesome they may be, have no place in formal, edited writing.

30. Errors in parallelism occur when one is thinking about content, not to worry about proofreading.

31. Its sad but true that omitting two apostrophes in one sentence interrupts a readers comprehension.

32. A curtain type of word is likely to be misspelled—as this sentence shows.

33. Their are some writers who ignore there proofreading skills on easily confused words.

34. Unintended humor occurs when you here one word but put down another—as illustrated hear.

35. This sentence would be clearer with quotation marks, you may be murmuring to yourself.

36. To catch writting errors here, you should of looked at its verb and at each word.

37. The semicolon; not the comma, can join two closely related sentences, this rule is broken here.

38. There is various kinds of problems related to subject/verb agreement that deserves your attention.

39. The affect of careless spelling is hard to measure but definitely effects readers' attitudes.

40. And last but not least, clichés are a pain in the neck to read.

To score your proofreading pretest, compare your check marks against these answers. You get 2 points for each correct item.

1. *Misspelling* is misspelled.

2. *Capitalization* should not be capitalized.

3. There is a missing comma after *tricky*.

4. *You're* is misspelled.

5. The sentence fragment begins with *especially*.

6. The sentence has an extra *in*.

7. *Out* is omitted.

8. The *'s* in *reader's* is missing.

9. The ending on *creates* is omitted.

10 *Confused* should be *confuse*.

11. A comma splice appears after *error*.

12. A run-on sentence occurs after *run-on sentence*.

13. There is a missing comma after *clause.*

14. There is a missing comma after *compound sentences.*

15. There is an unnecessary comma after *commas.*

16. *While,* the wrong conjunction, should be *if* or *when.*

17. *Which,* the wrong relative pronoun, should be *who.*

18. *That put modifying clauses in the wrong place* should appear after *sentence.*

19. The subject of the sentence should be *writers,* not *dangling modifiers.*

20. *Their* should be *its.*

21. *A lot* is misspelled.

22. *Another* is misspelled.

23. There is an unnecessary apostrophe in *apostrophes.*

24. *To split infinitives* should be followed by *unthinkingly and repeatedly.*

25. *For granite* should be *for granted.*

26. *Arrive to* should be *arrive at.*

27. *Your* should be *his or her.*

28. *Slang-type stuff* is slang.

29. *Totally awesome* is slang.

30. *Not to worry* should be *not worrying.*

31. *Its* should be *it's,* and *readers* should be *reader's.*

32. *Certain* and *sentence* are misspelled.

33. *Their* should be *there,* and *there* should be *their.*

34. *Here* should be *hear,* and *hear* should be *here.*

35. There are missing quotation marks before *this* and after *marks.*

36. *Writing* and *should've* (*should have*) are misspelled.

37. The semicolon after *semicolon* should be a comma, and the comma after *sentences* should be a semicolon.

38. *Is* should be *are*, and *deserves* should be *deserve*.

39. *Affect* should be *effect*, and *effects* should be *affects*.

40. *Last but not least* and *pain in the neck* are both clichés.

TARGETING YOUR ERRORS

Your proofreading-pretest score gives you baseline data for teaching yourself to proofread. Look carefully at the errors you missed in order to see what gives you trouble. As you work with the sentence-combining exercises, be alert to these "target" errors.

The aim is to study each error *in context,* not as separate "rules" to be memorized. The purpose for recognizing and naming errors—then rewriting sentences correctly—is to help you understand comments that your instructor (or peers) will make on your writing in progress. Here are the major types of errors you'll be considering:

TARGET ERRORS

Usage

1. Sentence fragments
2. Lack of subject/verb agreement
3. Lack of pronoun/antecedent agreement
4. Incorrect word forms

Punctuation

1. Comma splices
2. Run-on (run-together) sentences

3. Omitted punctuation

4. Unnecessary punctuation

Spelling

1. Improper capitalization

2. Misspelled words in general

3. Misspelled sound-alike words

4. Improper possessives and contractions

While all of these proofreading targets are important, some are more important than others. In particular, try to eliminate punctuation errors such as the comma splice and the run-on sentence and usage errors such as the sentence fragment and improper subject/verb agreement. To most readers, these are major potholes in the road. Whatever headway you can make against errors in spelling, particularly of sound-alike words and possessives, will also help make your prose more readable.

In Exercise 6.2, some errors will probably be obvious to you, but others will require searching. Especially at first, you may find it helpful to team up with another person in class to spot and discuss errors. If you follow this self-teaching and peer-teaching process, your recognition of sentence-level errors (and their identifying labels) will improve rapidly.

Each sentence-combining cluster is followed by a problem sentence that contains *three errors*. Cover up the sentence-combining cluster as you study the problem sentence. Use the reading-with-care method described in this book's introduction to look for the errors. Put a check mark above each one you find.

Finally, using the combining cluster as your guide, rewrite the problem sentence correctly on the lines below. Double-check your rewritten sentence, looking for spelling, punctuation, or usage mistakes. Afterward, check your work against the answer key.

EXERCISE 6.2: PROOFREADING PRACTICE

1. Proofreading is a skill.
   It requires attention to detail.
   The attention is close.

PROBLEM 1. Proof reading is a skill that require close atention to detail.

REWRITE 1. _____

_____

_____

2. Try to concentrate mainly on sentence form.
   Do not concentrate on content.
   Do not concentrate on organization.

PROBLEM 2. Try to consentrate manly on sentance form, not on organization or content.

REWRITE 2. _____

_____

_____

3. Use a pacer card.
   You will discover something.
   You're able to slow down your reading.

PROBLEM 3. Using a pacer card you will discover that your abel to slow down your reading.

REWRITE 3. _____

_____

_____

4. Reading slowly reveals errors.
   Errors are at the sentence level.
   They would normally escape attention.

PROBLEM 4. Reading slowly reveal errors at the sentence level they would normaly escape attention.

REWRITE 4. _____

_____

_____

5. You already know your message.
   Your mind fills in.
   It overlooks surface mistakes.

PROBLEM 5. Since you all ready know your message your mind fills in, it overlooks surface mistakes.

REWRITE 5. _____

_____

_____

6. But readers do not overlook errors.
   The errors are in spelling.
   The errors are in mechanics.
   The errors are in usage.

PROBLEM 6. But reader's do not overlook errors in spelling mechanics, or Usage.

REWRITE 6. _____

_____

_____

7. Each error is an interruption.
   It breaks the reader's concentration.
   It provides a source of irritation.
   The irritation grows.

PROBLEM 7. Each error is an interuption that breaks the readers concentration. Providing a source of growing irritation.

REWRITE 7. _____

_____

_____

8. Major errors suggest something.
   The errors are at the surface level.
   The writing is out of control.
   It should not be taken seriously.

PROBLEM 8. Major errors at the surface level suggest that the writting is out of control and should not be taking serious.

REWRITE 8. _____

_____

_____

9. These errors include sentence fragments.
   These errors include run-on sentences.
   These errors include garbled sentences.
   These errors undermine a reader's confidence.

PROBLEM 9. These errors include sentence fragments, run-on sentences, and garbled sentences which undermine a readers confidance.

REWRITE 9. _____

_____

_____

10. But minor errors also send a message.
    The message is loud.
    The message is clear.
    It concerns the writer's carelessness.

PROBLEM 10. But minor errors also send a loud, clear message, it concerned the writers carelessness.

REWRITE 10. _____

_____

In checking your work on the preceding exercise, first note the proofreading errors. Give yourself one point for each error that you spot. There are thirty possible points for this exercise.

1. misspelling of *proofreading*, omitted ending on *requires*, and misspelling of *attention*

2. misspellings of *concentrate, mainly,* and *sentence*

3. missing comma after *card* and misspelling of *you're* and *able*

4. omitted ending on *reveals*, run-on sentence between *level* and *they*, and misspelling of *normally*

5. misspelling of *already*, omitted comma after *message*, and comma splice after *fills in*

6. unnecessary apostrophe on *readers*, missing comma after *spelling*, and capitalization error on *usage*

7. misspelling of *interruption*, omitted apostrophe on *reader's*, and sentence fragment beginning with *providing*

8. misspelling of *writing*, wrong form of verb (*taken*), and missing ending on *seriously*

9. misplaced modifier (*which undermine a reader's confidence* should come after *these errors*), omitted apostrophe on *reader's*, and misspelling of *confidence*

10. comma splice after *message*, switch in verb tense (should be *concerns* or *concerning*), and omitted apostrophe on *writer's*.

Now compare your ten rewrites with the ones that follow. Yours may differ in minor ways.

1. Proofreading is a skill that requires close attention to detail.

2. Try to concentrate mainly on sentence form, not on organization or content.

3. Using a pacer card, you will discover that you're able to slow down your reading.

4. Reading slowly reveals errors at the sentence level that would normally escape attention.

5. Since you already know your message, your mind fills in, overlooking surface mistakes.

6. But readers do not overlook errors in spelling, mechanics, or usage.

7. Each error is an interruption that breaks the reader's concentration, providing a source of growing irritation.

8. Major errors at the surface level suggest that the writing is out of control and should not be taken seriously.

9. These errors, which undermine a reader's confidence, include sentence fragments, run-on sentences, and garbled sentences.

10. But minor errors also send a loud, clear message concerning the writer's carelessness.

Now that you've completed a practice exercise, take stock of your proofreading skills. How does your performance here compare with your performance on the proofreading pretest? Are your proofreading targets coming into focus? Consult a usage handbook or your instructor if you have specific questions. If your school has a writing center, you may be able to arrange for tutorial help on editing and proofreading.

MORE DIFFICULT PROOFREADING

Let's move on to a more challenging task. All you know about the following exercise is that each sentence contains from one to five errors. Once again, cover up the sentence cluster, referring to its words only as you need to. Read the problem sentence carefully for surface errors, and put a check mark above each one. Rewrite the problem sentence on the lines below it. Afterward, consult the answers and score your work.

EXERCISE 6.3: A CAMP-OUT TO REMEMBER
(Proofreading)

1. The night wind howled.
   It swirled through a canyon.
   Campers huddled together.
   They joked about the storm.
   The storm has been predicted.

PROBLEM 1. The night wind howled, swirling through a canyon where campers huddled together, they joke about the predicted storm.

REWRITE 1. _____

_____

2. It came at midnight.
   Sheets of rain came down.
   The sheets were horizontal.
   The rain was icy.
   The rain was wind-driven.

PROBLEM 2. Coming at midnight, their was horizontal sheets of icey, wind-driven rain.

REWRITE 2. _____

_____

3. The big tents were the first to collapse.
   They had only recently been purchased.
   They trapped their occupants.
   The trap was temporary.
   The occupants were terrified.

PROBLEM 3. The big tents, which had only recently been purchased were the first to collapse. Trapping there terified Occupants temporarily.

REWRITE 3. _____

_____

_____

4. The smaller tents were stronger.
   Many were located under trees.
   The location was unwise.
   Their limbs came loose.
   They broke without warning.

PROBLEM 4. The smaller tents were stronger, however, many are unwisely located under trees who's limbs come lose without warning.

REWRITE 4. _____

_____

_____

5. Something happened by dawn.
   The campground was nearly deserted.
   The forest was calm.
   The forest was quiet.
   The calm and quiet were complete.

PROBLEM 5. By dawn the campground was nearly desserted. With the forest complete calm and quite.

REWRITE 5. _____

_____

_____

6. Left behind were tire tracks.
   The tire tracks were muddy.
   Left behind were stacks of firewood.
   Left behind were memories.
   The memories were soggy.

PROBLEM 6. Left behind was muddy tire tracks, stacks of firewood, and soggy memories.

REWRITE 6. _____

_____

_____

   Now compare your proofreading with the following answers. Give yourself one point for each error that you caught. There are twenty possible points for this exercise.

1. comma splice after *together* and omitted ending for *joked* (2 errors)

2. wrong form of *there*, no subject/verb agreement (*was* should be *were*), and misspelling of *icy* (3 errors)

3. missing comma after *purchased*, sentence fragment beginning with *trapping*, misspelling of *their*, misspelling of *terrified*, and capitalization error for *occupants* (5 errors)

4. comma splice after *stronger*, wrong verb tense (*are* should be *were*), misspelling of *whose*, wrong verb tense (*come* should be *came*), and misspelling of *loose* (5 errors)

5. misspelling of *deserted*, sentence fragment beginning with *with*, missing ending on *completely*, and misspelling of *quiet* (4 errors)

6. no subject/verb agreement (*was* should be *were*) (1 error)

   Now compare your revisions with the ones that follow. Remember, your rewritten sentences may differ from these and still be correct.

1. The night wind howled, swirling through a canyon where campers huddled together, joking about the predicted storm.

2. Coming at midnight, there were horizontal sheets of icy, wind-driven rain.

3. The big tents, which had only recently been purchased, were the first to collapse, trapping their terrified occupants temporarily.

4. The smaller tents were stronger; however, many were located under trees whose limbs came loose without warning.

5. By dawn the campground was nearly deserted, with the forest completely calm and quiet.

6. Left behind were muddy tire tracks, stacks of firewood, and soggy memories.

LOOKING BACK, LOOKING AHEAD

While "correctness" isn't everything in writing, it makes a difference in how readers regard your prose. So spelling counts. And so does punctuation. And so do conventions of standard usage. Errors are like discordant notes at your favorite rock concert—definitely not what you expected or paid for. Whether your errors result from carelessness or ignorance matters little to your reader; the point is that errors create unwanted, irritating distractions.

Editing and proofreading require thoughtful concentration. As we have seen, they are the final step in the revision/editing cycle—and a crucial one. Here, after all, is where you pull together all of your ideas, drafts, and revisions into a final paper, one ready for the critical, discerning eyes of your audience. Your draft is "shaped up"; now it's almost ready to be "shipped out."

When editing or proofreading, don't forget that these tasks demand a highly deliberate, focused kind of reading, not the high-speed skim you normally use with familiar material. Slow down your reading; whisper aloud. Before doing the exercises that follow, turn to the "Becoming Another Reader"

section of this book's introduction and review its four suggestions for reading with care.

You have almost passed the final hurdle in your internship.
Good luck with do-it-yourself prose surgery in the real world
of writing. Welcome to the Club.

DO-IT-YOURSELF EXERCISES

Please be prepared to share your work in class. Your instructor will provide suggested answers for Exercises 6.4–6.7. Use
Exercise 6.8 to make a personal application of your proofreading skills.

EXERCISE 6.4: GARBAGE GLUT
(Proofreading)

Directions: Read each of the following sentences, and spot
from one to three errors in each one. Check each error you
find, and circle the type or types of error from the choices
listed below the sentences.

1. Besides problems of global warming and polution of air
   and water, Americans now have an added concern, this
   is where to put our garbage.

   1A. Run-on sentence   1B. Sentence fragment
   1C. Misspelled word

2. Each year we throw away about 160 million tons of trash.
   On average, 3.5 pounds per Citizen every day.

   2A. No subject/verb agreement   2B. Sentence fragment
   2C. Capitalization error

3. This level of solid, waste production is twice that of our european counterparts, who's lifestyles are similar.

   3A. Misspelled word   3B. Capitalization error
   3C. Unneeded comma

4. Although recycling is gaining in popularity only about 11 percent of solid waist in the United States is put to use again.

   4A. Misspelled word   4B. Misplaced modifier
   4C. Missing comma

5. This figure compared with a 40% recycling rate in other industrialize countries, such as Japan.

   5A. Dropped word ending   5B. Wrong verb tense
   5C. Run-on sentence

6. Our biggest source of consumer waste—41 percent by weight—are in paper products; product packaging, computer printouts phone books, newsprint, and junk mail.

   6A. No subject/verb agreement   6B. Wrong punctuation
   6C. Missing comma

7. While we recycle about 30 percent of our paper products and 50 percent of aluminum beverage cans, we still cannot match Japanese citizens, which recycle over half their paper and 66 percent of there food and beverage cans. Not to mention 55 percent of their glass bottles.

   7A. Sentence fragment   7B. Misspelled word
   7C. Wrong word

8. Our second biggest source of solid waste—about 18 percent before recycling—come from organic matter as grass clippings and leaves, these could easily be recycled into mulch.

   8A. No subject/verb agreement   8B. Run-on sentence
   8C. Missing word

9. As for our recycling rates of glass and plastics, only about 10 percent and 1 percent respectfully.

   9A. Missing punctuation   9B. Sentence fragment
   9C. Wrong word

10. We americans have made progress in recent years in recy-
    cling our garbage, however much remains to be done.

    10A. Wrong punctuation   10B. Missing comma
    10C. Capitalization error.

EXERCISE 6.5: TOTALITARIANISM
(Proofreading)

Directions: There are two errors in each problem sentence
that follows. Circle and name the errors that you spot; then
use the lines below to write sentences that correct the errors.

1. Totalitarianism is a term.
   It is used to describe governments.
   The governments are authoritarian.
   The governments are repressive.

PROBLEM 1. Totalitarianism, this is a term used to describe
repressive, authoritarian Governments.

REWRITE 1. _____

_____

2. Nations create societies.
   The nations are totalitarian.
   The societies are highly centralized.
   The societies guide people's daily lives.

PROBLEM 2. Totalitarian nations create highly centralized
societies that guides peoples daily lives.

REWRITE 2. _____

_____

3. Freedoms are always suppressed.
   The freedoms belong to the individual.

The suppression is to achieve goals.
The goals are revolutionary.

PROBLEM 3. The individual's freedoms that are always suppressed to acheive revolutionary goals.

REWRITE 3. _____

---

4. Propaganda is a totalitarian tool.
   It mobilizes support.
   The support is political.
   It helps maintain control.

PROBLEM 4. A totalitarian tool, propaganda mobilizes political support, and helped maintain control.

REWRITE 4. _____

---

5. The second tool is brute force.
   It is used by governments.
   The governments are repressive.
   This force serves to intimidate citizens.

PROBLEM 5. The second tool use by repressive governments is brute force, this serves to intimidate citizens.

REWRITE 5. _____

---

6. State planners shape behavior.
   State planners shape thinking.
   They reward conformity.
   They punish individuality.

PROBLEM 6. State planers shape behavior and thinking; by rewarding conformity and by punishing individuality.

REWRITE 6. _____

---

7. Their offices create networks.
   The networks are elaborate.
   The networks are for spying.
   The spying is internal.

PROBLEM 7. There offices create elaborate networks for
infernal spying.

REWRITE 7. _____

_____

8. Such methods have been the norm in Russia.
   Such methods have been the norm in China.
   They have also been used by military dictators.
   The dictators are fascist.

PROBLEM 8. Such methods have been the norm in Russia
and China, they have also been used by Fascist military
dictators.

REWRITE 8. _____

_____

EXERCISE 6.6: HEART DISEASE
(Proofreading)

Directions: There are two errors in each problem sentence
that follows. Circle and name the errors that you spot; then
use the lines below to write sentences that correct the errors.

1. Each year 1 million Americans die.
   The cause of their death is heart disease.
   It is a silent killer.
   It strikes with little warning.

PROBLEM 1. Each year 1 million americans die from heart
disease, it is a silent killer that strikes without warning.

REWRITE 1. _____

_____

2. It is the result of abuse.
   We inflict abuse on our arteries.
   The abuse is from eating habits.
   The eating habits are unhealthy.

PROBLEM 2. Its the result of abuse that we inflict on our arteries form unhealthy eating habits.

REWRITE 2. _____

_____

3. Arteries become choked with fats.
   The fats are greasy.
   They become choked with cholesterol.
   They cannot carry adequate blood to the heart.

PROBLEM 3. When arturies become choke with greasy fats and cholesterol, they cannot carry adequate blood to the heart.

REWRITE 3. _____

_____

4. They become like sluggish rivers.
   The rivers are slow-moving.
   The rivers are clogged with silt.
   The rivers are clogged with debris.

PROBLEM 4. They become like slugish, slow-moving rivers; which are clogged with silt and debris.

REWRITE 4. _____

_____

5. Cholesterol is a prime culprit.
   It builds up in the arteries.
   It forms arterial plaques.
   These are a type of scar tissue.

PROBLEM 5. Cholesterol is a prime culprit because it built up in the arteries and forms arterial plaques, these are a type of scar tissue.

REWRITE 5. _____

_____

6. Arteries become less efficient.
   They are unable to supply oxygen.
   The supply is to the heart muscle.
   The heart needs oxygen to function.

PROBLEM 6. As arteries become less efficient, they unable to supply oxygen to the heart muscle, which need it to function.

REWRITE 6. _____

_____

7. Then the heart begins to die.
   Its death is from oxygen deprivation.
   Its work load increases.
   Arteries become even more clogged.

PROBLEM 7. Then the heart begins to die from oxygen deprivation this increases it's work load as arteries become even more clogged.

REWRITE 7. _____

_____

8. The seizure is known as a *heart attack*.
   The seizure results from such strain.
   The seizure is deadly.
   The strain is massive.

PROBLEM 8. The deadly seizure known as *heart attach* that results from such a massive strain.

REWRITE 8. _____

_____

EXERCISE 6.7: SCHOOL CENSORSHIP
(Proofreading)

Directions: There are two errors in each problem sentence that follows. Circle and name the errors that you spot; then use the lines below to write sentences that correct the errors.

1. Censoring books is an issue.
   The books are in school libraries.
   The issue is emotionally charged.
   Basic values are at stake.

PROBLEM 1. Censoring school library books is a emotionally charged issue because basic values are at steak.

REWRITE 1. _____

_____

2. Censors argue something.
   Schools have a moral responsibility.
   The responsibility is to screen books.
   The books might be objectionable.

PROBLEM 2. Censers argue that schools have a morale responsibility to screen books that might be objectionable.

REWRITE 2. _____

_____

3. They say something.
   "Censorship is justified."
   "Youngsters often make poor judgments."
   "These judgments are about what to read."

PROBLEM 3. They say, "Censorship is justified, youngsters often make poor judgments about what to read.

REWRITE 3. _____

_____

4. They have a belief.
   Censorship protects children.
   Protection is from "trash" reading.
   "Trash" reading can cause emotional damage.
   "Trash" reading can cause antisocial behavior.

PROBLEM 4. There belief is that censorship protects children from "trash" reading; which can cause emotional damage or antisocial behavior.

REWRITE 4. _____

_____

5. They also contend something.
   Children read "quality" books.
   They internalize moral values.
   The moral values are desirable.

PROBLEM 5. They also content that as children read "quality" books, they internalized desirable moral values.

REWRITE 5. _____

_____

6. Opponents take a stand.
   The stand is legal.
   It is based upon the First Amendment.
   The amendment was to the U.S. Constitution.

PROBLEM 6. Oponents take a legal stand, it is based upon the First Amendment to the U.S. Constitution.

REWRITE 6. _____

_____

7. They argue something.
   Children are citizens.
   They have constitutional rights.
   The rights are like those of adults.

PROBLEM 7. They argue that children, being citizens have constitutional rights like those of adult's.

REWRITE 7. _____

_____

8. These rights include a freedom.
   The freedom is basic.
   The freedom is to read whatever one wishes.
   The freedom is to read without censorship.

PROBLEM 8. These Rights include a basic freedom; to read whatever one wishes, without censorship.

REWRITE 8. _____

_____

9. They also say something.
   "A range of reading helps children."
   "They develop internal standards."
   "The standards are for 'trash'."
   "The standards are for 'quality'."

PROBLEM 9. They also say, "A range of reading helps children develope internal standards for "trash" and 'quality'."

REWRITE 9. _____

_____

10. They contend something.
    Censorship is repressive.
    It runs counter to basic values.
    The values are in a democracy.

PROBLEM 10. They contend that because censership is repressive, running counter to basic values in a democracy.

REWRITE 10. _____

_____

EXERCISE 6.8: PERSONAL APPLICATION

In this chapter we've focused on proofreading for basic sentence-level errors. In the exercise that follows, you'll identify errors in your own written work and then make the appropriate corrections.

The first step is to make photocopies of several paragraphs of your work in progress. Since our concern at this stage is sentence-level errors, not content, make sure to select writing that is fairly well along in the revision and editing cycle.

Proofread your work as carefully as possible. Make check marks above the items that you regard as errors; if you're uncertain about an item, put a question mark above it. After you've completed your first reading, ask a friend from class, a tutor from the writing center, or your instructor to help you proofread your paper again, line by line, using the same coding system. Try to determine whether the items you questioned are, in fact, errors.

After proofreading your work at least two times, preferably more, turn to the following classification scheme:

TARGET ERRORS

Usage

1. Sentence fragment
2. No subject/verb agreement

3. No pronoun/antecedent agreement

4. Incorrect word forms

Punctuation

1. Comma splices

2. Run-on (run-together) sentences

3. Omitted punctuation

4. Unnecessary punctuation

Spelling

1. Improper capitalization

2. Misspelled words in general

3. Misspelled sound-alike words

4. Improper possessives and contractions

Using the above classifications, tally your errors in the various categories. If you find errors that don't fit under these labels, create a category for *other* errors. Total your errors in each category.

Now count all the words in the paragraphs you've been analyzing. By dividing the errors in each category by the total words in the selection, you'll create percentage ratios. For example, if you misspelled 8 words in a 395-word selection, divide 8 by 395. This would mean you have a 2 percent error rate in this category. In other words, even with 8 errors, your paper is 98 percent correct.

As a final step in your computation, count up the number of errors in *all* categories and divide this number by the total number of words in the selection. Your answer will once again be a percentage. Now edit your paper carefully, correcting all the errors. Try to bring your paper to an error rate near zero.

Write a paragraph summarizing what you learned from this close analysis of your own errors. Which category, if any, seems to give you particular difficulty? Which errors, if any, do you repeat? What questions do you have about basic matters of usage, punctuation, and spelling? What advice would you give yourself concerning editing and proofreading?

Hand in your work from this application activity. Your packet of materials should contain the following: (1) a photocopy of your writing in progress with errors checked; (2) a tally of errors as outlined in the Target Errors Taxonomy; (3) computations of error rates per 100 words for individual categories and for all categories totaled; (4) an edited version of your text, with all errors corrected; and (5) a paragraph summarizing what you learned from analyzing your sentence-level errors.

 **PROSE SURGERY IN ACTION**

In learning to write, all of us acquire certain habits—ways of working—that are automatic. These habits include spelling, punctuation, and usage conventions. We don't acquire new habits overnight, especially if we've practiced mistakes for many years.

When Leslie Ann Pilling-Smoak decided to get serious about her writing errors, she adopted an approach that works well for many students, once their content is "shaped up" and seems ready to be "shipped out." She read aloud and *listened* to her sentences. She paid *attention* to corrections and asked questions about them.

Leslie realized that proofreading demands focus, which she had never really learned in her earlier schooling. She wisely decided to concentrate on her serious problems first— run-on sentences and comma splices, for example—before moving on to other errors. She checked herself during conferences. By narrowing her attention while proofreading, she made dramatic progress over several weeks.

Note the many improvements Leslie made while developing the following essay. By *caring* about her prose and turning to newspapers, magazines, and books for examples of correct usage and mechanics, she taught herself many of the basics of writing.

Here are the four symbols used in class and in conferences to prompt revision and editing:

+ = I like this [word, phrase, sentence].

√ = Please check this [word, phrase, sentence].

? = I don't follow this [word, phrase, sentence].

= Think about developing this part more.

Summer Camp
(Response Draft)

Well I went to Camp twice that summer before starting into Jr. High and memories (kind of) blend together now. I guess time has away of rewriting memories for us, maybe to suit us. The memories of camp were mostly good ones thou or at least I don't remember any bad ones.

punctuation

spelling

chatty tone

Camp always started on a Monday just like school and, yes, there was some sort of schedual, but for the life of me I can't recall it. It did have a structure of groups rotating activities during the day so everyone got a chance at crafts, games & lunch!

Camp was located at Clear Creek, Utah. Its a good drive past Soldier Summit to a 6th grader I would guess about 19 or 20 miles tho. It is a old school house located in town. The town is made up of small houses, I'd call them a miner's home because of the small narrow windows as not to let out the heat. Anyway the bus pulled up to an old school and we had arrived. I found

num-on

comma splice

read aloud

a big stair case directly in front of me and two classrooms on my right & two on the left, with two doorways on both sides of the staircase.

[*The above draft goes on to describe several camp experiences.*]

Summer Camp
(Conference Draft)

So you never went to a summer camp? You don't know what
cap you missed. I went twice the Summer before going to Junior High. The memories have since blended together now. I guess
↑voice time has a way of rewriting memories for us, maybe to suit us. Most of my summer camp memories are good. I guess I filtered out any bad ones.

✓tone   To begin this trip down memory lane I'll start at the school that housed the camp. It was an old school, I can't recall if it was brick but it had large windows in fours on each side of the double door entranceway with wide stairs leading inside.
you? As you enter, there is a large open hall somewhat like a large room in itself. Here you can go off into many directions. For instance the right side of the room has two high ceiling doorways empting into the shop classroom and then the kitchen,
      were
on the other side was the two sleeping rooms for the campers. The wall paint looked new but you could tell it was whatever they picked up cheap, but the wooden floors, however old, gave the place class. There was also a large stair case in the middle
read aloud of the room opposite of the entrance leading up to a landing

that had two (off shoot) stairs on both sides. At the bottom floor
there were shower rooms on both side of the stairs, while
the upper staircases went to a strange gym-like room. I say
strange because it lacked the typical stage, high ceiling and
basketball hoops.

This school didn't lack organization, but I guess with thirty
or so girls you could not afford to. There was a rotation system.
You were first put into sleeping quarters and then into a group.
It was your group which was important to know most of the
time, so you got to shop, and to play ping pong, and horse
shoes, and most importantly to lunch on time. Later in the
day we all came together for outings and games, which also
happened in the morning for the jog to the water towers. (And
not to forget who did the organizing and supervision of this
week of fun, the directors Mr. R, and Mr. Z.) I had two different
lady chaperons, both were proper but one out shined the other
in fun, she was Mrs. W.

[*This draft goes on to describe several camp experiences.*]

Social Training Ground

by

Leslie Ann Pilling-Smoak

What was the purpose behind going to summer camp? Was it
to have fun, or make new friends? Maybe it was to have new
experiences. While I often have wondered why my mom sent
me off the summer before starting junior high, I do have fond
memories looking back now.

The camp was housed in an old school, with large windows in sets of fours on each side of the double door entryway. Wide painted cement stairs led into a large hall. The right side of the room had two tall doorways, one opening into the shop and the other to the kitchen. On the other side were the two sleeping rooms for the campers. On the bottom floor there were shower rooms on both sides of the stairs. The large staircase in the middle of the room, opposite the entrance, led up to a landing, with twin stairways on both sides like a goal post. The upper staircases went to a strange gym-like room that lacked the typical stage, high ceiling, and basketball hoops.

This school had no lack of organization. When we got off the bus we were a group of thirty or so girls. We were first divided into groups of fifteen and then assigned to sleeping quarters. Then we were made up into teams of fives. The directors used a rotation system. My team was important to know so I could make my rotations to horseshoes, to shop, to ping-pong, and most importantly to lunch. It was a great lunch. I can remember the smell of the rolls cooking. Later in the day we all came together for outings and games.

The people who did the organizing and supervision of this week of fun were the directors. Mr. R, who was a short, slender man wearing glasses and balding, reminded me of Charlie Chaplin in motion. The other director was Mr. Z, who was a little taller and larger, with dark hair. He was assertive and talkative, often taking the role of "Big Cheese." I had two different lady chaperones. Both were proper but one outshone the other in fun. She was Mrs. W, a tall brunette who wore glasses and a big smile. The other woman was a tall slender blonde who wore black cat-eyed glasses. All of these people were teachers.

Mornings began with a jog to the water towers. On one occasion we gathered some of nature's treasures. They were for a plan of sweet revenge to a practical joke that had been played on the girls and Mrs. W by our male directors. On returning to camp we set up our lookouts and quickly began to sew the goodies into the camp directors' sleeping bags. It wasn't until late that night we found out who got the frog.

Frogs are standard summer camp equipment, I believe. I remember one was planted in the sleeping bag of a very "lady like" girl. It learned to fly in the dark when she found it, sending a few of us ducking for cover. The next morning we found it in the shower of a screaming camper. By the time we rushed to the rescue of the startled girl, the frog had escaped. If there is an afterlife, I don't want to be a frog!

Late nights are standard events at summer camp, too. One night I remember so well started with "Shiny Bubbles" for the second time. Our unexpected audience of one, Mr. R, clapped and then assigned us to our new sleeping quarters. I ended up by the foot of the stairs. Another slept by the shop door, and the space by the kitchen door was now occupied. The girl by the shop was in pitch darkness and was now crying. We all sympathized with her. I thought about where I had ended up and wasn't too happy either; so much for partners in crime.

My first campout is stamped in my memory as a sleepless night of adventure. We built our very own pack frame in shop classes. It resembled a section of narrow ladder. We were encouraged to decorate them, and I did mine in a camouflage style resembling a giraffe. With gear packed on our backs, we hiked most of the afternoon up to a clear spot somewhere in the mountains. We set up camp, had a campfire dinner, and listened to ghost stories.

The fun came after the early birds had turned in. A few of us sat up talking into the late hours of the night about our teachers and boyfriends. Suddenly the woman chaperone sat up and said something like, "You don't know anything," and then quickly lay down again. This startled us for we thought she had overheard us. We sat quietly for a few moments and then checked to see if she was awake. When we decided it was getting late and we should get some sleep, we all went to our tents.

I awoke to someone calling my name, but in the background there was a rhythmic sound, so I couldn't tell who. I looked around, but nothing made sense to me. Waking up a little more, I realized it was raining and I wasn't in my tent any more. Someone was standing over me laughing. They told me I had slid down the hill in the rain and I had better get up or be left in the storm.

The ride down in the Jeep wasn't much fun that night. Gear was piled to the top in the back seat, and in the front huddled three of us girls, all soaking wet. We crowded the driver as he gripped the steering wheel with white knuckles and maneuvered the vehicle in and out of ruts, all the way to the schoolhouse. Back at the school, we spent the rest of the night taking turns using the dryer to dry out our sleepingbags. The next day I felt like a zombie as I rotated through ping-pong, horseshoes, volley-ball, and badminton.

Memories of those crazy episodes do bring a purpose to my summer camp experiences. I did have the organized fun which was planned for me, but I got my own personal lesson as well. I learned about acceptable deviance. Camp was a safe social training ground. I tested rules and learned what happens when you break them. No, I didn't set out to break rules . . . I was just having fun like kids are known to do.

APPENDIX: GENERATING AND DRAFTING STRATEGIES

> *Nothing you write, if you hope to be any good, will ever come out as you first hoped.*
>
> —LIllian Hellman

You know the feeling—hopelessness and tension. Nothing is happening, and you don't know why. You face a writing deadline, but you don't know how or where to start. You're out of the chair, up and down, pacing perhaps—or maybe just morose, staring at a TV screen or the back of your hand or a refrigerator's stark interior. Your well of words has gone dry. You're down on yourself.

Your experience is not unique, of course. Everybody who writes has, at one time or another, faced the dry well and wondered how to "prime the pump." Since writing appears easy—the apparently simple process of stringing words from left to right in space—it's easy to criticize yourself when things don't go well. And it's tough to be creative and intelligent when you've just told yourself you're not.

Making writing happen is anything but simple. Even the basic writing tasks—summarizing an article, giving how-to information clearly, or providing support for your opinions—require inner direction before you set pencil to paper or fingers to the computer keyboard. This is because writing is two events at once! It's a physical event (transcribing) and a complex inner event (selecting, planning, judging).

The process of generating and drafting prose happens in the interplay between the **outer game** (getting words down) and the **inner game** (summoning up a shadowy world of feelings, ideas, intentions, and half-formulated plans). Clarifying your plans—at least to yourself—is a first step in making the process work. But how is this done?

This appendix should give you some basic ideas for starting and sustaining your first draft. Then you'll have the chance to apply what you've learned in a follow-up writing assignment. You can use this draft as raw material for the personal-application exercises found at the ends of Chapters 1–6.

So don't lose hope. As a student of prose surgery, you'll see how an appendix can give you reason to take heart.

SEVEN GENERATING STRATEGIES

This section offers some suggestions for what to do when "nothing's happening." Not all of these strategies will work for you, but almost certainly some of them will. These, after all, are tools for thinking—nothing fancy, nothing complicated. Find the ones that feel right for you, and let them become part of your regular writing routine.

Remember to return to these generating strategies when you revise, especially when you need to create additional material or reorganize what you already have. You use writing to think, of course; but thinking is also what causes writing to take off in new, adventurous directions. Writing *feeds* thought, which in turn feeds writing.

Talking. The process of "talking out" ideas can be a wonderful generating strategy. After all, talk is *easy*. If you're having a friendly conversation, for example, you don't usually do much planning. Each person "feeds" the conversation in a natural, unrehearsed way. In a sense, good conversation is like mountain climbing—with you and someone else working as a team, making sure that the summit is reached safely. As you climb, you gather "new views" together.

By having a listener for half-formulated thoughts, you can make decisions about what to say and how to get started on writing tasks. Imagine a coffee shop, for example, with you and a friend at a corner table, talking about how things are going on your assignment. As usual, you're stuck. Perhaps you're discouraged, feeling sorry for yourself and looking for sympathy.

> "Uh-huh. So what's it on?"
> "That's what gets me. I started off on one thing—I mean, doing all this reading, taking notes—but now I'm somewhere else. I mean, you'll never guess what I'd really like to write about."
> "Sex?"
> "No, that's your preoccupation, not mine."
> "Okay, so tell me."
> "Well, since you insist—"
> "I insist?"
> "Do you want to hear it or not?"
> "Read my lips—*an-ti-ci-pa-tion*."
> "Okay, it's like this—"

And off you go, trying to make your half-formulated plans clear to your friend. Maybe you pull a napkin from the holder and jot down some key words. Meanwhile, your listener's questions and nods of understanding and occasional frowns combine to help you clarify ideas in your *own* mind. The talk serves as a rehearsal for the writing you eventually do.

While there's a danger in talking *too* much—thus diffusing all your energy for writing—you're alert to this potential problem. And so is your friend, who pushes the check to your side of the table as your plan begins to take shape.

Listing. As one of the simplest, most powerful techniques for generating ideas and creating order, the list is already familiar to you. You probably use lists regularly for routine tasks like errands. In the context of writing, lists are usually made quickly—often in a few minutes or less—and they can be modified or rearranged with crossouts or arrows.

Typically, writing lists unfold *down* the page, mirroring the sequence of topics that you plan to write about. Of course, topics within lists can provide the headings for indented sublists. Here's an example of my first working list for this appendix, created over a minute or two.

Possible Generating Strategies

listing	talking (others)
clustering	reflecting (self)
questioning	notebook (log entries)
freewriting	reading
outlining?	skim
headings	study
categories	notetaking

Listing probably works best as a generative strategy when you know your material well. Generally, your first list will be a rough one—an array of related words put down in the order you think about them. Very quickly, however, you will probably create a second or third list, rearranging words in a new order.

Your order may be chronological—a narrative, say, or a step-by-step process description. Or perhaps you'll arrange a series of topics from simple to complex, easy to hard, or nasty to nice. Lists always have a theme of some kind just beneath their surface. Your writing intentions create this theme.

Clustering. The clustering approach taps creativity, imagery, and unusual associations. It helps you shift from a logical, left-brain mode of thinking into the playful, right-brain mode. The left brain approaches writing problems from an analytic take-it-apart perspective, but the right brain sees the world differently. Memories, metaphors, and personal meanings—all are grist for the right brain's association mill. Whereas listing is straightforward and orderly, clustering is unpredictable. Here's a sample cluster:

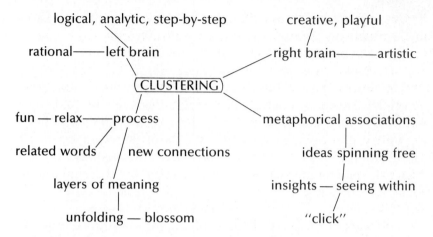

To cluster ideas, first of all relax. Put your topic in the center of a blank page, and let your mind make associations. Write down key words, a phrase at most. Have fun with the process by working fast. Connect related words with lines. Think of the cluster as a blossom, unfolding before your eyes.

Allow your brain to be as creative and playful as it wants. Watch the cluster emerge over a period of five minutes or so. As it does, you will sometimes feel a "click" of understanding—a sudden sense of insight into your topic. This click is magical because once you "see" what might be said, you've unlocked words within—and you're ready to write.

Sketching. Various kinds of sketches—with and without words—can help you plan your writing. Quickly making a rough "map" of your neighborhood, for example, would undoubtedly help you remember important places and events related to growing up. Such a map would help to focus and organize your thinking.

The same is true for a device like a "time line." A simple horizontal line with key events labeled on it can serve as the basis for a narrative or an autobiography—even, perhaps, for an analysis of your development as a writer. Here's a simple time line:

4th grade	11th grade	College
"The Nun"	"Term Paper Disaster"	"Learning to Write"

Other sorts of sketches also work. In analyzing characters in literature, for example, try drawing stick figures and labeling various conflicts. Such doodles can bring out your thinking. Does one character have sinister traits? Why not draw evil eyes and a pair of devil's horns? Use sketches as adjuncts to other strategies. Playful sketching, like other methods for brainstorming, can free up both language and ideas.

Finally, don't overlook the possibility of sketching connections among ideas. Even very complex relationships can be symbolized with circles, boxes, arrows, and other visual models. For example, the flow-chart of writing process that opens this book (see p. 6) helps to clarify a complex recursive event. The process of thinking through the details of that diagram helped me generate the words that followed.

Freewriting. Scribbling words as they come to mind—unplanned, nonstop writing—sometimes leads to unexpected breakthroughs in the logjam called *getting started.* Try to get the flow going—and don't worry about what's being said or how it relates to the topic or assignment.

The task of keeping your pencil moving or your fingers dancing on the computer keyboard somehow frees your mind from the usual worries about content, organization, and "correctness." In a sense, freewriting diverts your attention so that you can sneak into the "house of writing" by the back door. It's a good approach when nothing else works.

If you can't think of anything to say while freewriting, simply write that thought a time or two. You'll grow tired of it, of course, and your mind will turn to other things— why, for example, you can't find anything to say. Here's an example:

> Stuck like usual. In a rut, unable to move. But different this time. I know what I could do, but I don't see how pieces of the appendix fit together. I mean, I'd like to use headings for this section. But how to get started— some kind of *hook*. Talk about the problem of nothing happening? Frustration, nervousness, the tension of pacing back and forth, trying to figure it out? Might work—I don't know. I could lead into the headings, the point-by-point

sections on generating ideas. Maybe worth a shot. I've got to start somewhere.

As you can see, the freewriting approach can help you think about where you're going with a piece. But equally important, freewriting can help you solve content problems. Getting words down on paper—fast—often releases a powerful problem-solving voice within. Think of it like listing, clustering, or any other approach to generating ideas.

It's important, of course, not to confuse freewriting with a finished piece. A stream-of-consciousness draft may make sense to you but remain a mystery to others. Freewriting amounts to shorthand—personal, telegraphic in style, often cryptic. It gets your engine revving, but you don't hand it in as a finished product.

Questioning. For informational writing, questions can be a very powerful tool. Questions have energy behind them, particularly when you ask them thoughtfully: *Who's my audience here? What's my main purpose for this section? How can I get the reader's attention? What key points do I want to make? How should I sequence the points? Do I need to provide some background or context? How long is "long enough"—and "too long?"* Questions like these—and a host of content questions related to your topic—can get you started.

For this appendix, one question I asked was, How many generating strategies should I include? I debated between an encyclopedic approach and a personal one. If I took the encyclopedic approach, it would mean including everything I'd ever heard or read about that might possibly work; the personal list would include only methods that have worked for me and my students. Since it didn't seem right to describe strategies I hadn't used, I finally chose the personal approach. Asking a question forced me to decide on a plan.

By listing questions your reader might have, you create a natural sort of text organization. Try putting questions on note cards and then using these cards as organizers for both your research and your writing. Questions can easily be converted into topic sentences that lead into paragraphs. Sometimes, too, you might leave questions as headings or as paragraph openers to engage your reader. You don't want to overdo this device, but it can work for a change of pace.

Finally, of course, questions focus your reading and your search for "something to say." Quite likely you will find yourself reading in a special way whenever you face important writing tasks—your radar attuned to ideas and information that might prove useful in your writing. In other words, once you achieve focus for your writing, you have a lens through which you filter the world.

Outlining. For some documents—particularly long ones such as research papers or major reports—outlining your major points, section by section, can be a real benefit. Because the writing of a major paper takes place over days, weeks, or even months, it's helpful to have a road map to return to.

Not that this plan has to be a straitjacket, of course. In the process of drafting and revising your paper, many new ideas will probably occur to you and the map will change. That's understandable—even desirable. An outline is merely a tool for thinking. The point is that advance planning frees up mental space for actual writing.

The note-card technique described above can help you develop a topic outline. Put key words or phrases on separate note cards, spread them out on a large surface, and sort them into categories. After the cards are organized into piles, try to see sequences for the stacks of cards. Finally, transfer your working plan (arranged before you) into an outline or flowchart.

Here are three possible formats, among many, for the topic of outlining. Each has potential to serve as a road map.

Outlining

    A. Useful for major documents

    B. Like a road map, not a straitjacket

    C. Note-card technique
       1. key word and phrases—separate cards
       2. categorize and sequence
       3. create outline

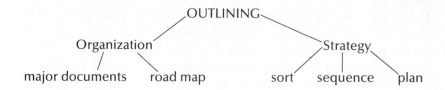

Outlining Intro $\longrightarrow$ Outlining How-to

why use it	separate note cards
road-map analogy	categorizing, sequencing
not a straitjacket	transfer to working plan

Which of these formats is best? It depends on your personal preference. What counts is having something to return to—and a secure place to work from. Most people find that an overall plan reduces the fear of writing. Equally important, a plan gives you something to *work against*—a set of ideas you can change as insights occur, a way to decide where you want to go as alternate routes suggest themselves.

In changing a plan, you may feel a sense of adventure. You've taken a detour off the mind-deadening interstate, and perhaps you're edgy about what you'll encounter next. Still, there's comfort in knowing you can always get back to the paved highway if the back road proves to be a dead end. Having a conventional route as a backup can help you relax as you explore uncharted territory.

SEVEN DRAFTING STRATEGIES

This section deals with **drafting**—the process of getting words on paper (or on the computer screen) so that you can rework them. What follows are ideas that may help you relax and write productively. Above all, remember that successful drafting results partly from your attitude—and partly from giving yourself enough time to be successful.

The right attitude, I think, is a balanced one. On the one hand, you need to realize that the task requires work. On the other hand, you need to understand that problems may result if you take yourself too seriously—demanding perfection, for example. The right approach balances work with play. It's saying to yourself: "Well, let's see what happens."

Knowing Yourself. Where do you write best? What tools do you prefer? Do you need to set deadlines for yourself? Such questions are hardly trivial if you're serious about developing writing skill. By developing an awareness of your needs and preferences—the places, tools, and conditions that help you work effectively—you increase your odds for success both in drafting and in doing the prose surgery that follows.

If procrastination is one of your habits, it's time to grow up. Putting off a writing task serves only to heighten your anxiety. Know that fear is generally your enemy, not your ally. It interrupts your thinking, diminishes your creativity, and makes you less productive and intelligent than you might otherwise be. Give yourself a break by budgeting plenty of time to develop a solid draft. Reward yourself for not putting it off.

For me, drafting often works in places like McDonald's where nobody hassles you, the coffee refills are free, and there's a low level of background noise. I prefer pens with laserlike tips. I have an aversion to slick, clay-coated paper and a fondness for cheap note pads, especially soft yellow ones. How about you?

Sitting Still. It's tough, but there's no other way. To develop a draft, you have to sit still long enough to create some momentum. In other words, with generating work behind you, stick with your writing a while—pushing yourself to get words down and disciplining yourself *not* to engage in revision, editing, or self-criticism. The point of the writing process, remember, is to work smarter, not harder.

Though sitting still may not be easy at first, it does come with practice. Set goals for yourself—writing for four minutes, then seven, then ten. Work up to longer periods until you feel comfortable transcribing your inner voice. Try transcribing sentences you've just read—say these. How many words can you hold in your short-term memory? Can you extend this number with concentration? Listen to the cadence of sentences as you practice transcription.

You might think of such exercises as the kind of strength-building work that weight lifters, runners, and dancers engage in. When you make progress toward your goal of concentration, reward yourself with something you enjoy. Sitting still for a sustained period will help you achieve a feeling of relaxed attention—a readiness for writing.

Finding Your Reader. Writing requires you to imagine someone out there with whom you're communicating. This is true whether the reader is familiar or unknown. If you're writing to a schoolchild, for example, your imagination helps you decide on vocabulary, sentence length, and general approach. On the other hand, if you're writing a job application, you'll picture another reader and make a different set of decisions.

You'll probably find it useful to think of your reader as an individual, not as part of a faceless group. Why? Because reading is always an individual act, not a group experience. The task of imagining your reader becomes tricky when your text will be read by people with different levels of background knowledge or sharply divided opinions. Yet it must be done if you hope to develop a draft.

In drafting this section, for example, I thought about a certain kind of student, one of college age. This reader is partly myself thirty years ago and partly a composite of older students in my writing classes. I see this reader as intelligent and motivated, yet suspicious of easy answers and nervous about the complexity of writing. "Don't talk down to me," this reader says. "Be clear and honest and help me write."

Finding a Writing Voice. With your reader in mind, you face another important decision—the "voice" of your text. Think of **voice** as the person you project through your words. Does a cozy, familiar voice seem right for your research project? Does a cool, analytic voice fit the requirements of expressing sympathy? Does a snarling, cynical voice seem appropriate in requesting a loan for college tuition? For your writing to work, the voice has to fit.

Difficulties with drafting can often be traced to problems of voice. Getting clear on a voice for your text means understanding your aims and your reader's probable needs. To do this, try putting yourself in your reader's shoes. What sort of voice would *you* like to hear speaking through the lines of the text? If the writing task is a class assignment or an essay exam, picture yourself as an overworked instructor looking for clear topic sentences and richly detailed support. You'll probably use a voice that is direct, crisp, and to the point.

With your voice may come a semiconscious strategy toward the subject at hand. This strategy is sometimes evident in word choices or in the general style of a text. In this section on voice, for example, my strategy was to define the concept through multiple examples.

Finding Points of Departure. Even with a reader and a voice in mind, you'll find that sentences don't always flow into place. Don't be alarmed. Instead, try writing a list of **points of departure.** These are possible opening sentences for your draft. Sooner or later, you'll find one that interests you. It's this one, of course, that you need to extend and elaborate.

Think of point-of-departure sentences as "trail heads" to enter the wilderness of writing. Each trail takes you through different terrain, so it's hard to say which one to take. But the point of backpacking is to enjoy yourself, not to worry about the best route. Or think of point-of-departure sentences as different routes for the daily commute. You don't wait all day for a freeway to clear when there are other roads that will get you to your destination. The point of commuting is to get there, not to worry about the best route.

Opening sentences set the direction for everything that follows. I like to fiddle with openers, trying to make adjustments in wording or structure. While I'm never sure how these adjustments will work out, I simply can't go on until the point of departure *feels* right. I try to write fast after departure, but I'm not always successful. My usual strategy is a back-and-forth one—writing, reading; writing, reading—to develop momentum for my draft.

Working Fast. As noted above, you need to begin where you can develop some writing momentum. If that means beginning in the middle, so be it. It's far better to *start somewhere* than to dither for hours, wondering how to get started.

Having begun at a point where you can get something done without too much struggle, you try to work fast.

In drafting this appendix, for example, I visualized a "chunk" of introduction followed by two "chunks" of follow-up material—one section on generating ideas and another on drafting them. I drafted "Seven Generating Strategies" first because it seemed straightforward and manageable; however, if the section on drafting strategies had seemed easier, I would have started with that. I didn't worry about how the pieces fit together because I regard that as revision— a later step in the process.

Working fast means trusting yourself to make sense. One or more generating strategies serve to get you percolating; then you create a rough draft, focusing on the flow of meaning and not on the details of wording and punctuation. When you feel yourself falter, simply reread what you've written, listening to your inner voice and imagining yourself as your reader. Trust your own instincts first; then get help from other readers.

Changing Direction. For minor roadblocks, the reread-and-write strategy usually works. For major obstacles, however, you'll either need to generate additional material or take a major detour. So pause. Pull back from your writing. Ask yourself, What seems to be the problem here? Am I merely out of gas or do I need a new road map? Review your original plans, however crude and tentative they may be.

Suppose you're in the middle of a draft and a fresh road map has begun to emerge. Unfortunately, you're not sure where it's headed or whether you can follow it. The new plan is vague in your mind—a blurry sense of possible paragraphs you might write to get through the present impasse. So what should you do? Stick with the old plan, or move to a new one? Play it safe, or take a chance on an unknown direction?

My advice is to sketch the new plan and then take a break from drafting. If possible, let your subconscious mind work on the new plan overnight. Take a fresh look at it the next day. If the new road map still seems exciting, then your decision is made—you change direction. On the other hand, if your enthusiasm for the new plan has waned, you're probably better off sticking with your original idea.

YOU AS A WRITER: A CASE-STUDY ASSIGNMENT

How did you learn to write? What experiences shaped your present attitudes and your beliefs about writing? To what extent do your present skills as a writer grow out of earlier events? These are the central questions for this writing assignment.

Such questions are worth pursuing because if you understand your own development as a writer, you're likely to develop further insights into basic writing processes, including revision and editing. For this assignment, you are your own source material.

Your goal for this assignment is to prepare a kind of case study of yourself as a writer. Think back to your memories of learning to write—the lessons you learned both in and out of school about how to communicate on paper. Some lessons may have been positive, others painful. Whatever their effect, they all contributed to your development.

You might begin by taking notes. The idea is simply to list your thoughts as they come, letting the memories flow. If you can't remember at first, don't worry. Your unconscious mind will go to work on the problem. You will find yourself beginning to recall unexpected bits of the past at odd moments as you relax or dream.

Jot down these fragments—situations, scenes, images—in a notebook. In other words, spend some time simply collecting "stuff about writing" from your memory. Later you can do the sorting and selecting. From that sorting process will come a first draft of your case study.

Here are some questions to get you thinking and making notes:

1. Who or what was the earliest influence, either positive or negative, on you as a writer? How did that influence affect your attitudes toward writing? Your beliefs about yourself as a writer? Try to identify later influences as well.

2. How have you felt over the years about the task of writing? Have there been changes that you could graph

on a scale? How do you feel now? How would you *like* to feel? How would you assess yourself as a writer at this stage of your development?

3. What are your writing "behaviors"? That is, how do you get the job done? When and where do you write best? How much could you (and can you now) write in one sitting? Do you need to pace, eat, read aloud, talk aloud, rewrite as you go? Do you have special writing tools? What are your working habits? Where did you learn them?

4. To what extent have you written (and do you write now) just for yourself? For other people? Does having an audience help or hinder you? What about writing for a teacher audience? What kinds of writing have you enjoyed most and least? Why do you think this is so?

5. If possible, go back to your love letters, files, scrapbooks, or diaries to collect samples of your writing. What are some distinctive features of this writing? How can you account for the changes over time? What can you say about your "voice" as a writer? Your sense of purpose, tone, subject, and audience? Your commitment to writing?

The point about notetaking is to gather a rich data base from which to develop a draft. Let your mind take you from early memories to more recent ones. Think about the teachers from your past, assignments you turned in, love letters you wrote, contests you won (or should have won), and the grades or other feedback you received.

Since this is a case study of yourself as a writer, you should support your various points with details from remembered experience. Because your reader has no knowledge of your experience, you will need to describe and narrate past events in some detail, showing their present significance. The real purpose of this assignment, remember, is to help you learn more about your own writing processes.

How long should this paper be? Try for a draft of three to five pages. This will provide you with enough raw material for some serious revising and editing work.

LOOKING BACK, LOOKING AHEAD

The introduction to this book showed you a way to work smarter, not harder, when you face writing assignments. The diagram for a two-stage model of the writing process looked like this:

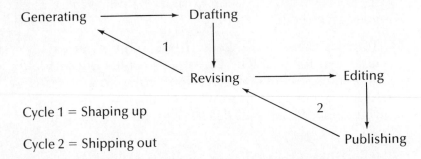

While most of this book dealt with strategies for revising and editing, this appendix has focused on ways to generate ideas and get them down in draft form. A case-study writing assignment that can serve as raw material for revising/editing practice concluded the appendix.

Let's end at the beginning. After all, learning to write is a lifelong process—like learning to live. There are rich sources of knowledge within, and finding them means learning to listen, learning to question, learning to think. Experience provides our text, and text does the teaching.

And the bottom line?

Take time to pay attention.

INDEX

INDEX